The Apples and Orchards of Worcestershire

(Including Pears)

A County Pomona

Wade Muggleton

Apples and Orchards of Worcestershire, Wade Muggleton

Published by Aspect Design 2017
89 Newtown Road, Malvern, Worcestershire, U.K.

Printed and bound by Aspect Design
Tel: 01684 561567
E-mail: allan@aspect-design.net

All Rights Reserved.

Copyright © 2017 Wade Muggleton

Wade Muggleton has asserted his moral right to be identified as the author of this work.

The right of Wade Muggleton to be identified as the author of this work has been asserted in accordance with Section 77 of the Copyright, Designs and Patents Act 1988.

This book is sold subject to the condition that it shall not, by way of trade or otherwise, be lent, resold, hired out or otherwise circulated without the publisher's prior consent in any form of binding or cover other than that in which it is published and without a similar condition including this condition being imposed on the subsequent purchaser.

A copy of this book has been deposited with the
British Library Board

Cover Design Copyright © 2017 Wade Muggleton
Front cover photograph, May Queen in the author's garden
Back cover photograph, Jones Seedling from the author's collection

ISBN 978-1-912078-64-6

Contents

Introduction	1
What constitutes a variety?	2
Trains, Cider and Worcestershire Orchards	4
Are Heritage Varieties Important?	7
Varieties of Worcestershire	9
The Lost Varieties	75
Pears	79
Clues from History	85
Orchard Stories	87
The Home Orchard	92
Aftercare	93
The Future	94
Acknowledgements	95
References	96

Hope Cottage Seedling

Introduction

"So how come you are so interested in Apples?" she asked, to which I paused and, after thinking about it for what seemed like more than a few moments I replied, "Well everyone knows a lot about something, for some people it's football, soap operas or cars I guess for me it's just apples".

But on deeper reflection apples are surely interesting because each variety has its own story, the tale of from whence it came, who found or bred it, its popularity or lack of, in short each of our apples is a little piece of social history... a little bit of the locally distinct.

The concept of a Pomona, a book on fruit, more often than not apples, had its heyday in the late 1800s when the esteemed men and women of august societies recorded and catalogued varieties of the day with great earnest.

The Herefordshire Pomona published in 1870 by the Woolhope Naturalists' Field Club is perhaps the greatest and most famous of such works - a true monument to the dedication of those who compiled it.

There has seemingly never been a Worcestershire Pomona where all the varieties of the County are recorded together in one place. This is an attempt to rectify that and to capture those snippets and stories, characteristics and appeal of the apples of this County, once so famous for its orchards.

Wade Muggleton 2017.

What constitutes a Variety?

A variety is simply an apple that has been studied, named, listed and propagated. Every apple grown from a pip is potentially a new variety and all those you see growing randomly at the side of the road or on waste ground are new varieties, just ones which have not been studied or named. For every apple grown from a pip is different due to its genetic variation and the fact that it has been cross pollinated. Thus a seedling apple is 50% the parent tree which bore it and 50% whatever the bees or other insects pollinated it with, and that could have been a cooker, an eater, a cider or a crab apple. As a result when growing apples from pips it truly is a case of "You never know what you're going to get".

This is why in order to cultivate a variety we have to take cuttings and vegetatively propagate them by grafting or budding, thus ensuring that the new tree will produce apples identical to its parent. An apple grown from a pip will produce apples but they will not be the same as the apple they came out of. They will be a cross, in exactly the same way that breeding cattle, dogs or daffodils produces different crosses.

This is fundamental to understanding the growing of apple trees and their propagation; Many people still presume young apple trees are merely grown from seed (i.e. pips). Apples will happily grow from seed, just look along the sides of our dual carriageways and motorways but they will be new varieties of unknown character and reliability. In order to get a known variety you require a grafted tree.

Bred or Found
A named variety starts out in one of two ways, it is simply found as one of those seedlings, deemed to be of some merit, given a name and some cuttings are taken, thus replicating it.
Alternatively a variety might be bred, when nurserymen or enthusiasts take two noteable apple varieties, isolates them in say a greenhouse, and then when in blossom they cross pollinate them with a paint brush or rabbit's tail, thus ensuring the resulting pips are a known cross. This still does not guarantee a good apple, but works on the basis that two good varieties intentionally crossed may produce an even better variety. The pips from the resulting apples are then propagated and grown on over a number of years to see if they do indeed produce a new variety of worth. Within the following pages are descriptions and photographs of those apples which are

deemed to have originated in the County of Worcestershire either found as wild grown seedlings, or they were specifically bred by nurserymen or residents of Worcestershire by crossing known varieties.

A selection of local varieties harvested from the author's garden

Trains, Cider and Worcestershire Orchards

What you might wonder have steam trains got to do with Orchards? Well in the case of Worcestershire a lot! For the coming of the railways was perhaps the greatest influence on the story of the County's orchards. The train really did change the nature of fruit growing in Worcestershire. Before the mid 1800s virtually all orchards would have been small affairs, attached to family farms, small holdings and gardens, primarily supplying the household and perhaps selling a small surplus to the immediate locality. They would have consisted of a wide range of early, mid and late season varieties designed to give a steady supply through the season, as well as good numbers for keeping through the winter.

Around 1850 onwards when the railway network spread into the countryside, entrepreneurial land owners spotted the opportunity for large scale orchards where by the fruit could be picked in the morning, put on a train at lunchtime and be for sale in the urban centres the following morning. From 1870 onwards it was boom time and large scale orchards sprang up throughout the county to supply the burgeoning populations of Birmingham, the Black Country and beyond.

Prior to this, distribution of a perishable product on a large scale was simply not possible. So the history of the railway is the reason Worcestershire went from small diverse orchards to larger less diverse orchards. As for why Worcestershire? Well, soils, climate and topography all suited fruit production, so once the railway arrived with its distribution possibility it became ideal orchard country.

Even with the coming of the large orchards, diversity would still have been important to supply a range of varieties to the market at different times; many old orchards would have had a couple of rows each of several different varieties, ripening successively through late summer and autumn, to supply the market, so as one variety came to the end of its season another was ready to replace it. A notion all but lost today with refrigerated storage and global distribution.

The seasonal aspect of the orchard year was an integral part of many people's lives; picking provided seasonal employment and sale of the harvest made up a considerable part of the yearly farm income, as such huge effort was put into maintaining the trees in good health, and in particular, bird scaring. Our feathered friends being the greatest enemy of the fruit grower.

As a county Worcestershire had regional specialisms, the Teme Valley was largely apple production, the Wyre Forest and surrounding area was big in cherries, whilst the Vale of Evesham was more latterly renowned for plum growing, and this specialism made sense. Neighbouring holdings could share pickers and distribution costs and bird damage was minimised due to the abundance of crop all at one time; there is only so much one bird can eat per day.

The great social aspect of orchards over many centuries was cider, the drink of the rural masses. It was made on a vast scale and pre the 1930s most farms made their own, it was even said that the reputation of your cider would influence the desire of pickers and seasonal labourers to work for you. If the farm up the road had a better cider they would offer their services there instead. Further back in history farm labourers were part paid in cider with a daily allowance of several pints. For much of history it was safer to drink than the water, the alcohol content killing off any pathogens. After the second world war, when the country was on its knees the big brewing companies sent agents around the country offering cash to poor farmers to buy up their cider presses, which were then deliberately destroyed. Thus the larger companies effectively stifled the smaller competition and so monopolised the market. It is perhaps only today with the growth of artisan cider and perry makers that we are finally seeing a reversion to smaller scale local production again.

Orchards are a strange habitat: completely man made and the study of old maps will show how they move around the landscape; coming and going in different phases of history, they are not ancient habitats in the way a woodland might be. In many places vast orchards were planted in the 19th century, existed for 100 years or so and are now completely gone.

The demise of our orchards was swift and driven by a range of factors. Two world wars changed the nature of the rural work force forever, the decline of the railways and the growth of road distribution meant it was no longer necessary for orchards to be near railway lines and then in 1973 when Britain joined the EU a flood of cheap imported fruit was for many the death knell of an already struggling industry. The grubbing out of orchards was subsidised and they vanished on a vast scale; as many as 85% have gone in Worcestershire alone.

Today when it comes to apples most people only know a handful of supermarket varieties, Gala, Pink Lady, Cox, Braeburn, Golden Delicious. A tragedy when we have over 2000 British varieties of apple alone. Here in the County there were over 30 exclusively Worcestershire apple varieties, all except one (Worcester Pearmain) are now rare, never to be seen in a shop. How many people have ever tasted a Hope Cottage Seedling, a Tupstones, a Chatley's Kernel or King Charles Pearmain?

Today the demands of the supermarkets, with their obsession with uniformity, year round distribution and refrigerated storage, mean the locally distinct and the characteristics that went with them have been lost. However in the last 20 years there has been a small grass roots level resurgence of interest in the locally distinct, in knowing where food comes from and traceability. People have become interested in the plants, trees and food of their area and some of these rare varieties have become available through specialist nurseries and promotional schemes. It is hoped that in some small way, this volume contributes to furthering that interest in our local varieties here in Worcestershire.

Apples on display at Tenbury Applefest

Are Heritage Varieties Important?

It is easy to assume that these old or heritage varieties fell from favour and began to disappear simply because they weren't that good and were thus replaced by more modern varieties that have come along. In a few cases this may be true, but there are still hundreds of heritage varieties that have a huge amount going for them, be it disease resistance, keeping quality, hardiness, fantastic flavour or wonderful appearance. Indeed a varied collection of heritage varieties on a small holding or large garden scale can provide you with a wonderful and diverse range of apples for about 9 to 10 months of the year.

The downfall of our heritage varieties is seemingly that they do not meet the uniform standards of all growing to an exact size, shape and colour that the supermarkets are today obsessed with. The likes of William Crump, Tupstones or May Queen may never be grown on a mass scale to adorn the supermarket shelves, but they have much to offer us when grown in our gardens, small holdings and allotments.

There is good sense in selecting a variety that is local to your patch; by its very nature it is going to be suited to the local conditions. If you do some research and read up, you can find a variety that keeps well through the winter, or one that comes early and will give you fresh apples in August. The range and diversity is extraordinary, there is a saying that "if you don't like apples you simply haven't found the one that is for you", for there are crisp apples, soft apples, sharp apples, sweet apples, bitter apples, ones that look like lemons, ones that taste of honey, there is even one that supposedly tastes of coffee!

Modern supermarket apples are of course cold stored for availability 12 months of the year, whereas in the days before refrigerated storage keeping quality was a huge factor and some varieties were grown for this quality alone. Although not a County variety Scotch Bridget was once widely grown in Worcestershire, as they will keep until April or May. Whilst the incredibly rare Worcestershire variety called Tupstones can be picked in late October and come March they look and taste exactly as they did the day you picked them, they appear to have an extraordinary keeping quality. They simply aren't all the same size and shape.

This concept of year round apples is a very modern one, for they would once have been eaten as a seasonal crop, the earliest like

Gladstone and Beauty of Bath ripen in late July or early August going through to the late varieties picked in November or even December and stored through the winter, probably running out by April or May at the latest and then there would not have been any apples until August again. This is a pattern I follow today, for I grow 100 odd varieties and when the last of the keepers have run out we simply don't have apples until the season begins again. Like asparagus, tomatoes and runner beans, perhaps the humble apple should also be a seasonal crop, looked forward to, enjoyed and then gone for another year.

There are countless stories of great characteristics in our heritage varieties. In effect modern varieties are a bit boring, they are mass produced, sweet and juicy and in truth a bit all the same. Our heritage varieties have texture, flavour, a range of sweetness through to sharp, an extraordinary diversity of appearances, a range of seasonality and keeping qualities. They are part of a living heritage. I am often asked what I would recommend, to which I reply "well I don't know what you like, my favourites are probably unlikely to be yours," so the key is to go out and track down and try as many varieties as you can and, when you find the one(s) you like, go and buy a tree of that variety from a specialist fruit tree nursery.

So if you are planting anything please do plant something special, something local to your patch and be part of keeping Heritage apples alive.

Display of Apples at a Community Apple Day

Varieties of Worcestershire

Within the following pages are contained descriptions and photographs of those apples and pears which are deemed to have originated in the County in some form; that is they were found as wildings grown from pips or they were specifically bred by nurserymen or residents of Worcestershire.

Any such list is speculative and open to debate, and indeed there are those who deplore the whole notion of County Lists, but each variety has a particular story to tell and a historical association with place. A number of these varieties are claimed as Worcestershire by virtue of having been introduced by local nurserymen; as the County was once rich in fruit nurseries and this gives the county a good list. However the actual seedling or bred stock could well have originated elsewhere before coming into the hands of Worcestershire nurserymen, and nationally some varieties are claimed by more than one county.

In compiling this list I acknowledge the work of Common Ground and their Apple Map of 1993, which really set in motion this whole notion of the locally distinct and seeking out the varieties of each county.
This list is made up from the Common Ground list of Worcestershire apples plus considerable additions from information acquired from local research. The four Counties of Worcestershire, Herefordshire, and Shropshire and Gloucestershire were once all rich fruit growing areas and there is inevitably a slight degree of overlap with one or two varieties claimed by two Counties. We should not argue over specific varieties for it is the story as well as the merit of the variety that we are recording here.

Betty Geeson

This obscure and now rare cooking apple is believed to have been introduced in 1854 by a Mr Davies of Pershore. However its name suggests a possible link to Betty Geeson of Belvoir who, some claim, raised it from a pip, in which case it would actually be a Leicestershire variety in true origin. It was grown extensively in the Midlands as a commercial variety in the 19th century until superseded by better commercial varieties, most notably Bramley.

It appears to have a sluggish growth pattern so some nurseries propagate it on M25 rootstock in an attempt to give it an extra boost. The apples themselves are a flat round and have a light green / yellow skin which, in a good summer, can turn a red flush. They store well, keeping until Christmas, but develop a slightly greasy skin in late storage. The flesh has a yellowish appearance and is sharp, juicy and crisp when first ripe, softening with age. When cooked it has a rich, sweet texture and holds together in slices.

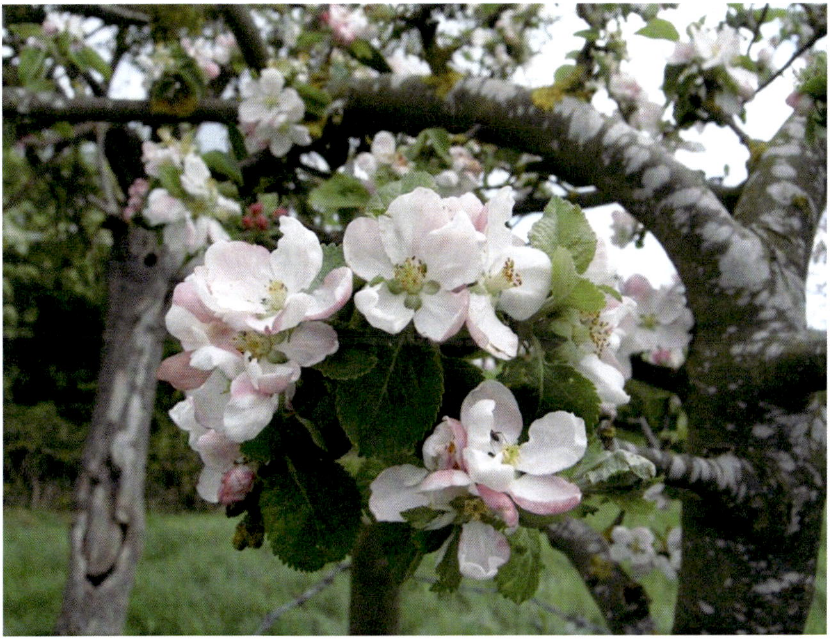

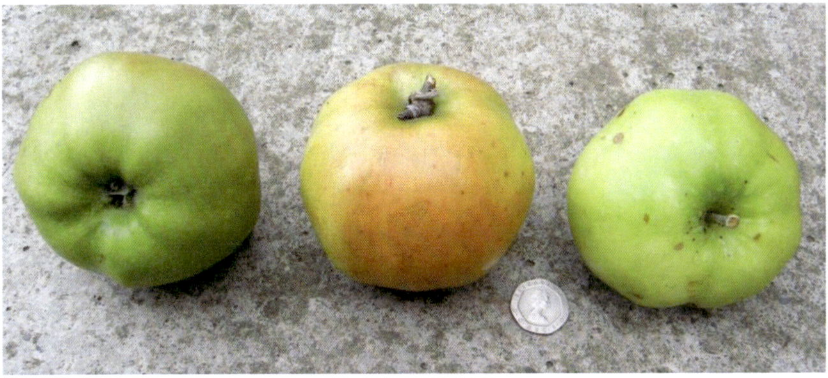

Captain Tom

This distinctive large dual purpose variety has an angular shaped fruit, and a distinctively large and unusually beautiful pink blossom.
It was introduced by F P Matthews nursery of Tenbury Wells, who obtained it in the 1980s from Geoffrey Knight, a descendant of the 18th century pomologist Thomas Andrew Knight. Its exact origin is unclear but it seems to have been long grown in the area since the Marcher Apple Network (MAN) described it as 'an old farm apple' and gave it a working name of Downway Costard as they had found it growing in 3 locations. Initial DNA analysis however, suggests it is possibly the same apple as the variety Castle Major.

Something of a dual purpose apple as it eats well and is a good culinary apple. Picking time October and will store until December.

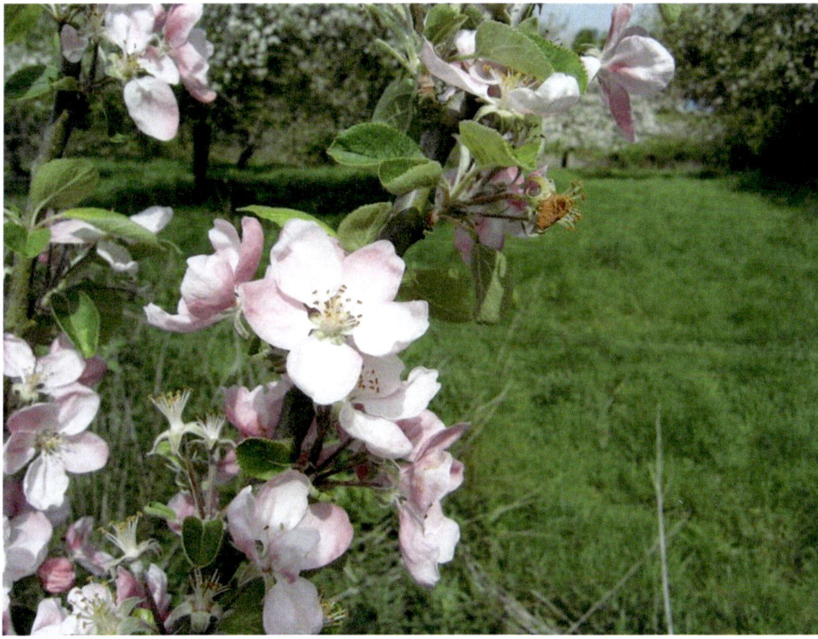

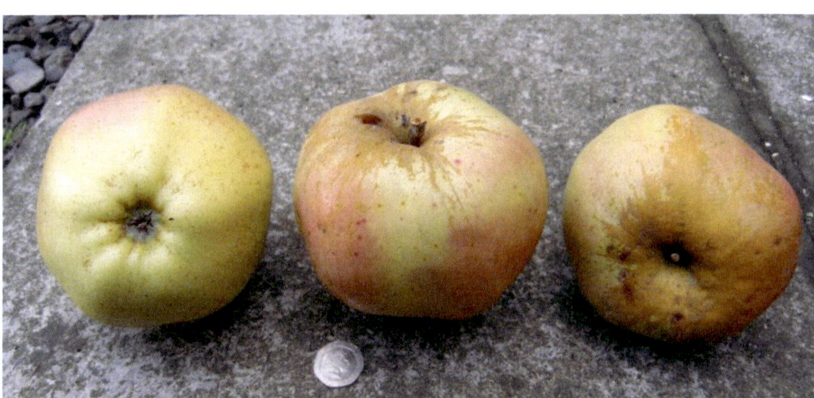

Catshead

An old English culinary apple, whose origin is unclear but is considered a possible Worcestershire / Herefordshire apple. It is recorded as far back as the 1700s; another cooker that has been surpassed by more modern reliable varieties. It takes its name from a supposed resemblance to a cat's face, the fruit come in a vast range of sizes and odd shapes, a very angular and oblong apple, with skin that becomes greasy with storage. They will keep beyond New Year, the flesh is white, sharp and cooks down to a good puree as well as being a good baking apple.

Despite being heavy croppers, disease resistance appears questionable with the trees susceptible to scab and canker and the fruit to bitter pit. Definitely a worthy addition to a collection but there are undoubtedly finer culinary apples to be had if looking for a single tree for a garden.

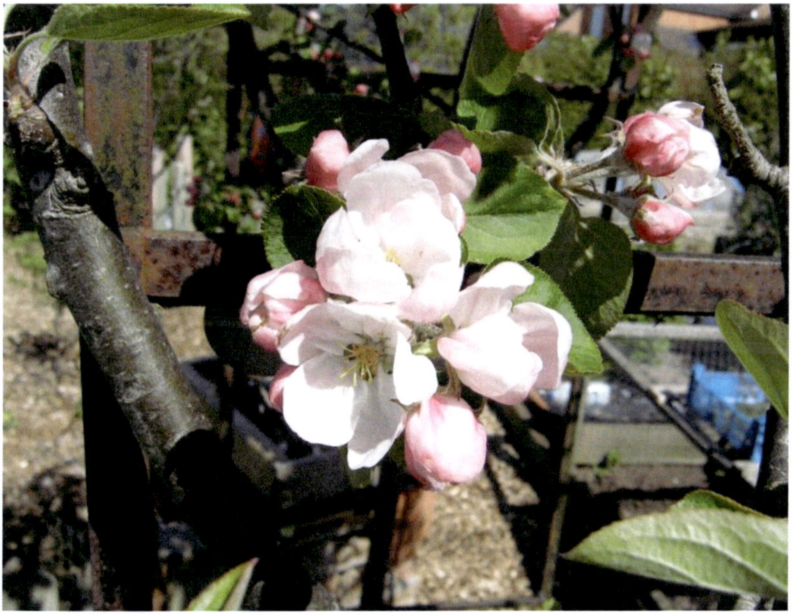

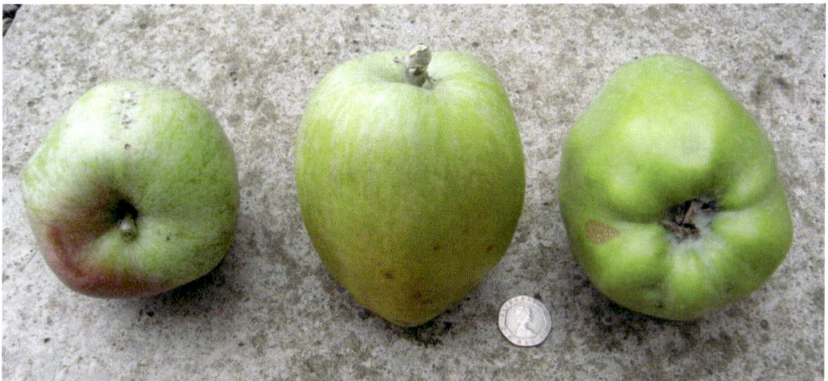

Chatley's Kernel

A onetime lost variety of the county, until it was rediscovered in the 1990s by local farmer Peter Weekes. An apple of the Ombersley / Chatley parish, Peter followed up stories his father told about the village apple, eventually finding four remaining old trees. Working with the Marcher Apple Network, the rediscovery was confirmed and graft wood was taken, so restabilising the variety.
A medium sized dessert / dual purpose apple it stores well and eaten fresh has a crisp, juicy and slightly sub acid flavour. From observation it seems to have a biennial cropping tendency producing a huge crop one year and very little the next, before another huge crop.

Chatley's Pippin
Is a red version (or Sport) of Chatley's Kernel, this apple could possibly be a result of a colour variation developing within the original variety, and in a good hot summer the Chatley's Kernel will ripen to be as red as the Pippin, making them all but indistinguishable
There is anecdotal evidence of there being two supposedly different Chatley Apples: a Green one and a Red one. So for that reason it is included it here, although recent DNA analysis proves them to be identical.

Colwall Quoining

A dessert apple, received by the National Fruit Trials in 1949 from Tenbury Wells, Worcestershire. Although the village of Colwall is just in Herefordshire on the western side of the Malvern Hills, meaning its true origin is across the border in the rival county of Herefordshire.

Fruits have very distinct angular ridges and the quoining is said to mean corners indicating this angular nature. There are several other quoining varieties in this group of apples, all possessing the same angular shape. The fruit has crisp coarse flesh with a sweet sub acid, slightly nutty flavour. Keeps until November.

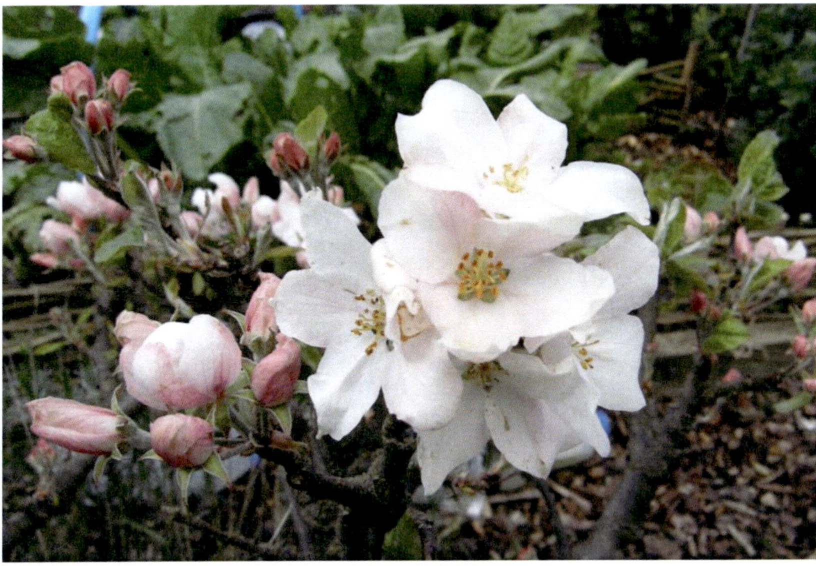

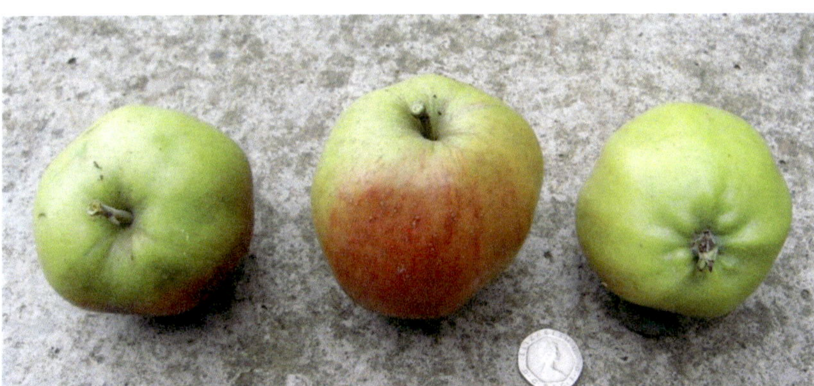

Dewdulip Seedling

This green culinary apple was sent to the National Fruit Collection from Tenbury Wells in 1946 by a Rev Lee, the then vicar of the parish of Eastham in the Teme Valley. The original tree is believed to have grown on an area known as the flats, common land in Eastham.

A medium to large apple, the shape is flat, rectangular to conical and slightly ribbed at the eye and on the body. The skin is green to yellow with occasional pale orange to red flush, russet dots, sometimes in patches. The flesh is coarse but soft with a sweet sub acid flavour. The season is late, keeping well into the winter. The trees are partial tip bearers.

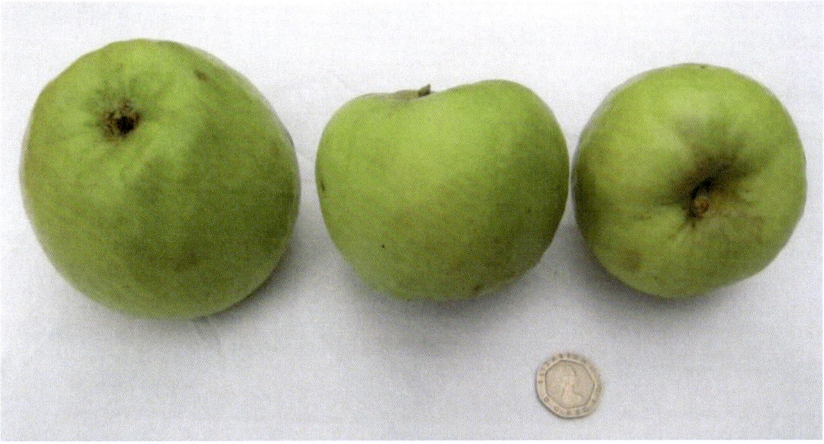

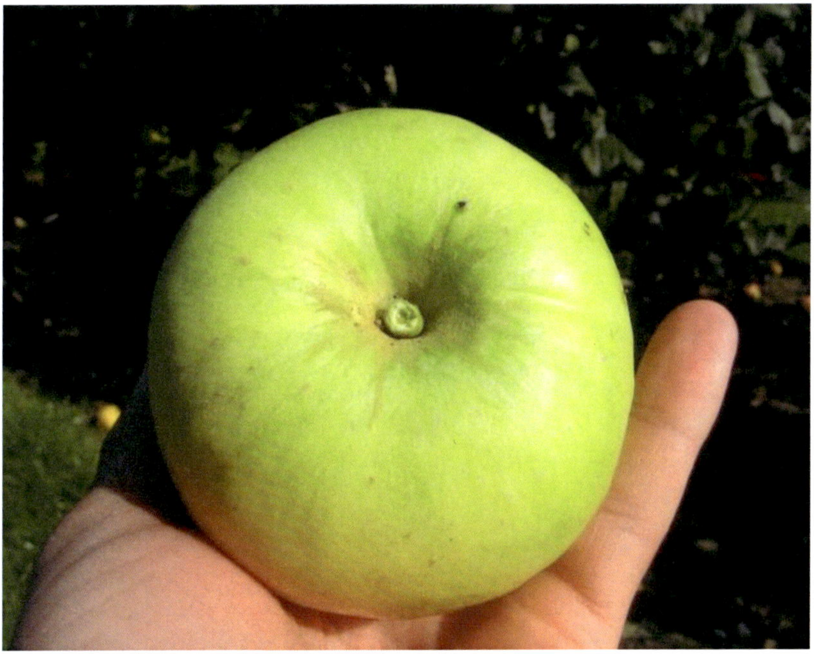

Dick's Favourite

Who Dick was and why this was his favourite is sadly not known. But this culinary apple is thought to have been raised in the late 1800s by Carless, foreman at Rowe's Nurseries in Worcester.

A large, flat round apple with a strong red flushing over a green skin when fully ripened in a good year. Fruits are crisp with an acid flavour which cooks well.

Like so many other regional culinary apples it was almost certainly superseded by more commercial and prolific varieties like Bramley. Beyond this, very little else is recorded about this variety.

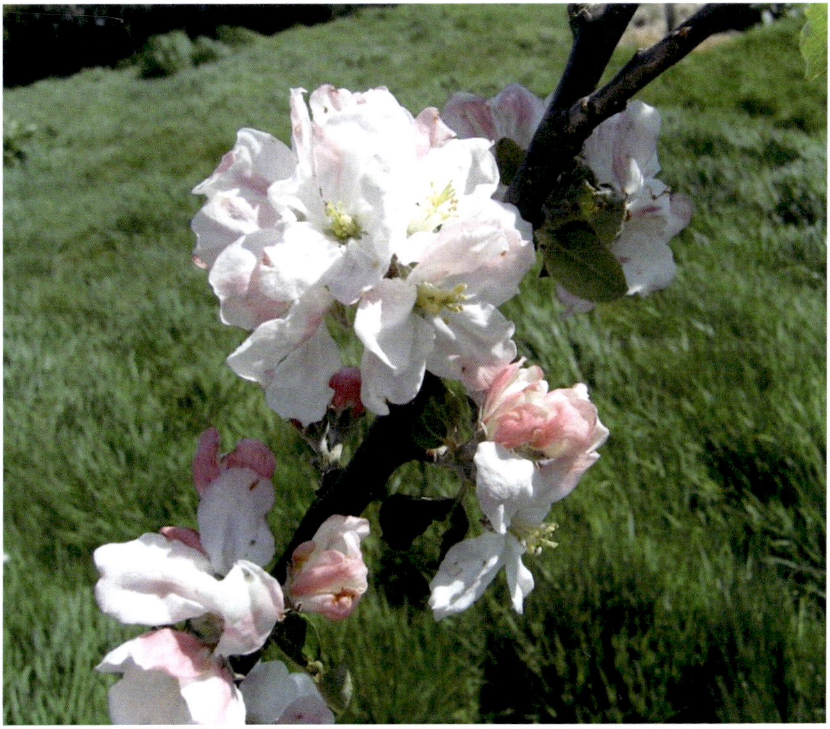

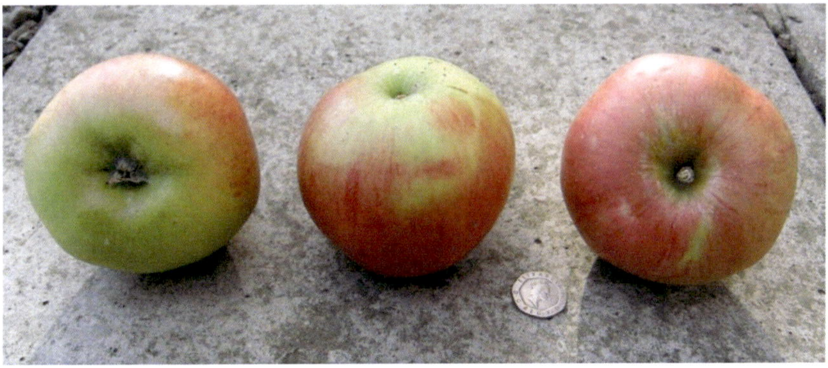

Doddin

Also sometimes pronounced daddin this is an unusual apple mostly found around Redditch. The apples are bright green, smooth skinned and turn somewhat yellowish as they become ripe in late July / early August. No bigger than a golf ball when fully mature and slightly elongated, juicy and sweet. Ripening early they do not keep so should be consumed quickly. It is claimed they were usually eaten whole including the core.
The tree is claimed to grow freely on its own rootstock and makes a small, slow growing tree of a bushy nature, often with multiple stems. It is tolerant of wet and heavy clay soils.

Around 2009 there were only a handful of known trees, perhaps less than twenty, all in the Redditch area. Since then a few others have been discovered and new grafted trees made available, so the population is on the rise.

Almost certainly an obscure wilding that someone decided to propagate. It is hard to see its appeal beyond its very early nature, when it would have been a source of fresh fruit very early in the season, before most other varieties were ready.

Edward VII

Another of the older culinary apples that was no doubt displaced by Bramley. It dates from 1908 when it was introduced by Rowe's Nursery of Worcester. Having been first recorded in 1902 it is thought to be a Blenheim Orange X Golden Noble and won an RHS award of Merit in 1903.

As a tree it is hardy, with a good resistance to scab, and crops on spurs if not renowned for being prolific. It is late to flower and thus could be a good choice for a frost pocket. It is ripe for picking in Mid October with a use season from to December to April, thus historically valuable for keeping.

Makes a good garden tree due to a neat upright growth pattern, although it can be slow to crop especially on the larger rootstocks.
The flesh is white, firm and juicy, if a little coarse, beneath a thick skin and it cooks down to a good puree.

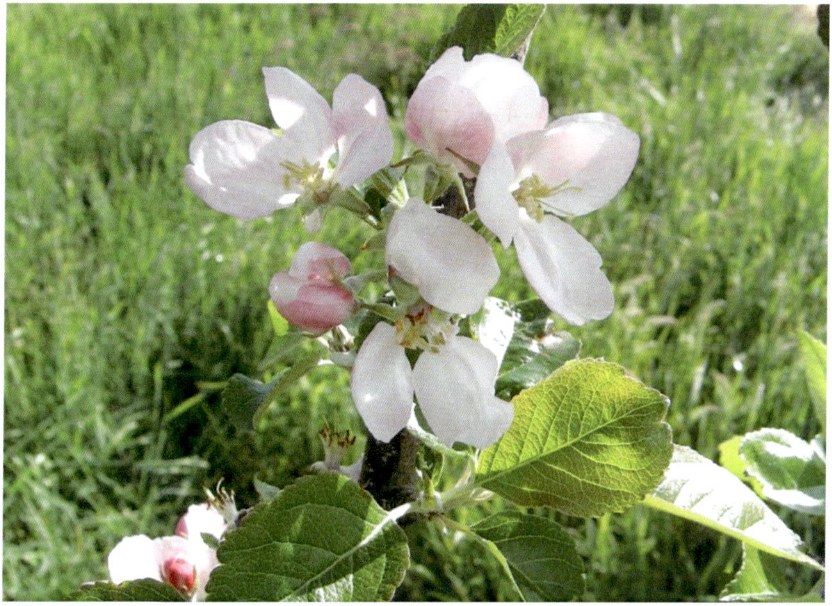

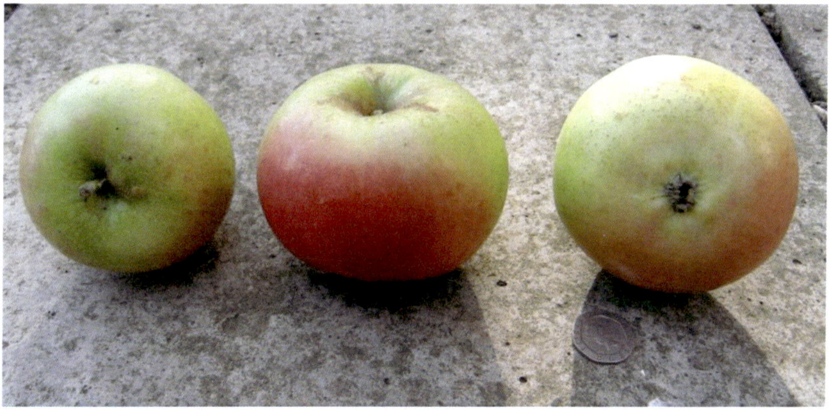

Gladstone

This apple was introduced in 1868 by a Mr Jackson of Blakedown Nursery, Kidderminster and was named Jackson's seedling as it was said to have been a chance find, presumably by Mr Jackson himself. In 1883 it was awarded a First class certificate of merit by the RHS and was subsequently renamed Mr Gladstone after the Prime Minister of the day, the Mr being later dropped and more recently simply known as Gladstone.

It is one of the earliest apples of summer in a good year. Being ready as early as late July it would historically have been a welcome first fruit of the season, however, like many early varieties its keeping quality is almost non-existent and is only really any good eaten straight from the tree.

The fruit is very white, sweet and has a perfumed fragrance, although the flesh is soft and fluffy by comparison to crisp modern

apples and as such may not be to the immediate taste of the modern consumer.
As a tree it can be vigorous on a larger rootstock and is tip and spur bearing, sometimes with a biennial tendency. One for the collector, but due to the total lack of keeping quality not one you would want vast quantities of. Interestingly it was crossed with many others to presumably try and replicate its early season nature, while improving on flavour and keep ability, thus it is parent to several other well known varieties. An apple to be enjoyed as the first of the season.

Green Purnell

Supposedly an old variety, yet one of which little is known or recorded. It was introduced to the National Fruit Trials in 1945 being said to be from the County of Worcestershire. It can still be found in a few old orchards in the Region and is sometime referred to simply as Purnells.

The fruit viewed in August seems a bright green medium sized dessert, yet by late October develops rich red and orange streaks resembling almost a completely different apple. Fully ripe by November it will keep until January. The flesh is firm, creamy and fine, juicy and sweet.

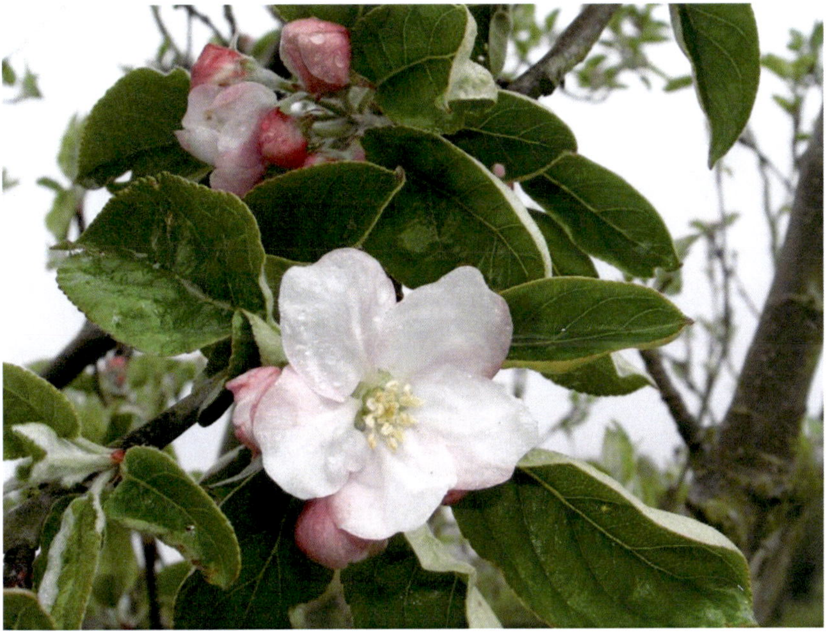

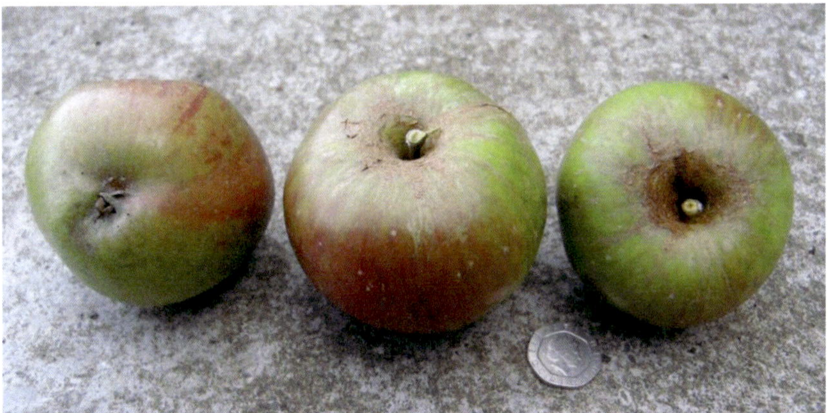

Haughty's Red

This mid to late season red dessert apple was first sent to the National Fruit collection in 1946 from Tenbury Wells. Believed to have come from the parish of Kyre, the original tree (now long gone) is said to have grown in a field on the riverside. The Haughty's were a family at Kyre wood and Old Hall Rochford, from whence the name is presumed to have come.

The apples are medium in size, shape is intermediate, rectangular with the apex sometimes broader than the base, convex to slightly straight. Ribbed at the eye and prominently on the body. The skin is yellow flushed with orange, red and stripes of crimson, with some russet. The flesh is soft and slightly coarse, cream in colour and has a sweet flavour.

33

Herefordshire Russet

A modern dessert russet, raised in 1975 by Mr Hugh Ermen, Faversham, Kent. Introduced in 2003 by Frank P. Matthews Ltd., Tenbury Wells, Worcestershire.

As a tree they are strong, upright and seem well suited to heavier and wetter soils, thus making it a good all rounder.
They are ripe from late September onwards and will store from October to January. The flesh is hard, crisp and juicy, creamy white with a slight greenish tinge. It has the nuttiness of other russets, yet with an added juiciness; a good example of the best of modern apple breeding with some good traditional characteristics. Obviously not by name or origin a truly Worcestershire variety.

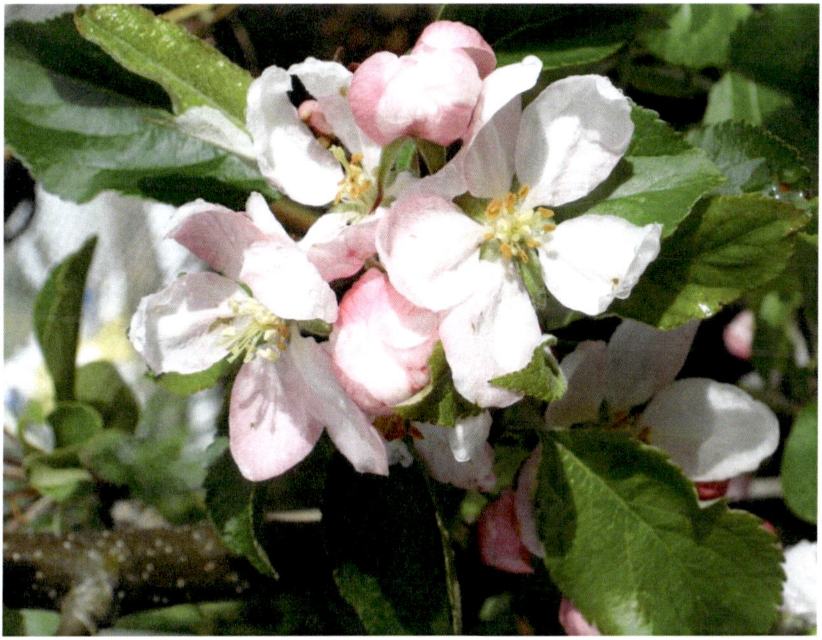

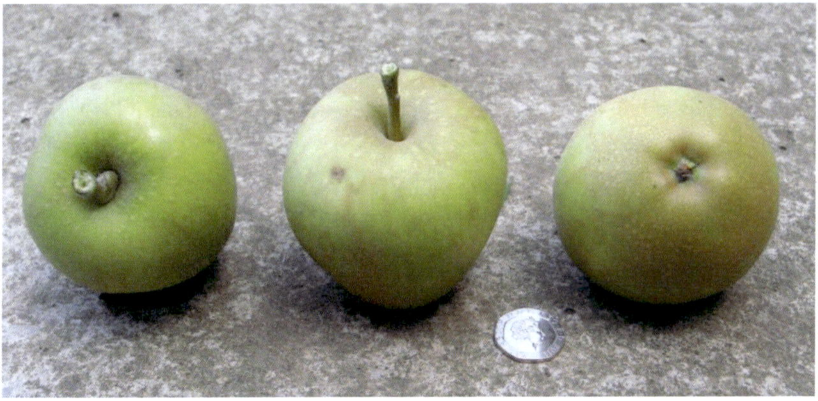

Hope Cottage Seedling

An early season dessert apple, raised in 1900 by Mrs Oakey at Hope Cottage, Rochford near Tenbury Wells. In line with other early season varieties is eats beautifully straight from the tree. Fruits have firm, fine flesh with a sub acid flavour, but do not keep, going soft and past its best in a few weeks.

A great tree to have as one to enjoy fresh in September, but not a variety you would want a whole orchard full of.

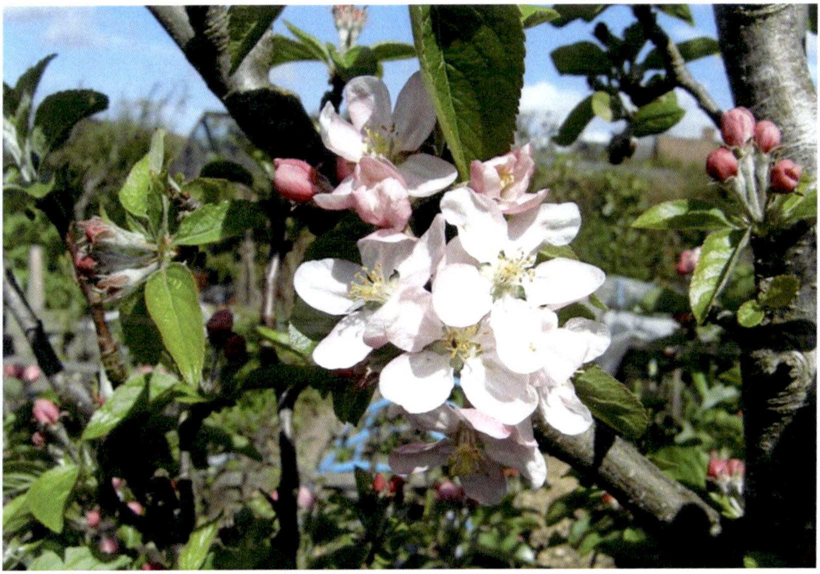

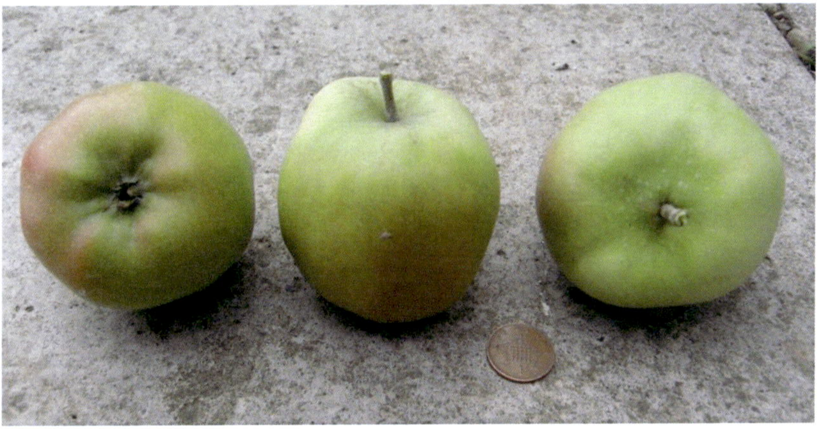

Jones's Seedling

This apple is claimed to originate in the Teme valley area of Worcestershire; an early season apple with a skin of red streaks over a yellow-pale green base.

The apples seem to be of varying shapes and sizes on the same tree. It appears to have fallen from favour after WWII and is now extremely rare and localised to the St Michaels and Tenbury Wells area. It is almost certainly not the same Jones' Seedling as the one listed in the National Apple Register as being a late season variety from Epsom in Surrey (1938). Jones being a common name and 'seedling' a common pomological reference it could well have been a seedling that was replicated by grafting in only a very local area. There is anecdotal evidence of it being grown in several orchards in the Tenbury area in the 1930s but beyond this there are seemingly no other references.

The Teme Valley Apple Group located one old tree in 2013 on the farm of member Jon Edwards of St Michaels, from which graftwood was taken, so perhaps saving it from being lost.

King Charles' Pearmain

A dessert apple said to have been raised by a Charles Taylor, a blacksmith of the village of Rushock in Worcestershire in 1821, claimed by Hogg in 1876 to have been introduced commercially by nurseryman John Smith of Worcester. Fruits have a golden base colour covered by a thin brown russet, the flesh is firm and crisp with a sweet and rich flavour. It will keep through Christmas and well into the New Year. It was at one time claimed to have been widely grown for the markets of Birmingham.

It is also known as Rushock Pearmain. Whether the King Charles naming or association comes from Charles Taylor or a Royal reference seems un clear, the Herefordshire Pomona claims it was known for a time as Charles Pearmain, suggesting the former. Robert Hogg actually referred to Rushock Pearmain and King

Charles Pearmain as being two separate varieties in his Fruit Manual of 1884, it is now accepted that they are the same variety.

King Coffee

This is another of those varieties of which little is known or recorded yet has the fascinating claim to be the coffee flavoured apple, making it a must for any collection. It was exhibited in 1934 at an RHS Fruit Conference and three years later an E.W. Hobbies (a horticultural Instructor for Worcestershire County Council) supplied graft wood to the National Fruit Trials, claiming it to be an old Variety of the County.

A dessert apple, the fruit matures to a dark maroon colour when fully ripe, beneath which the flesh is greenish white, sweet and juicy with sadly only the merest hint of coffee, if discernible at all. Picked in October the fruit will keep until Christmas. As a tree it is one of the latest apples to break bud and often still resembles bare sticks whilst other varieties are fully in blossom, however this characteristic makes it a worthy choice for frost prone sites.

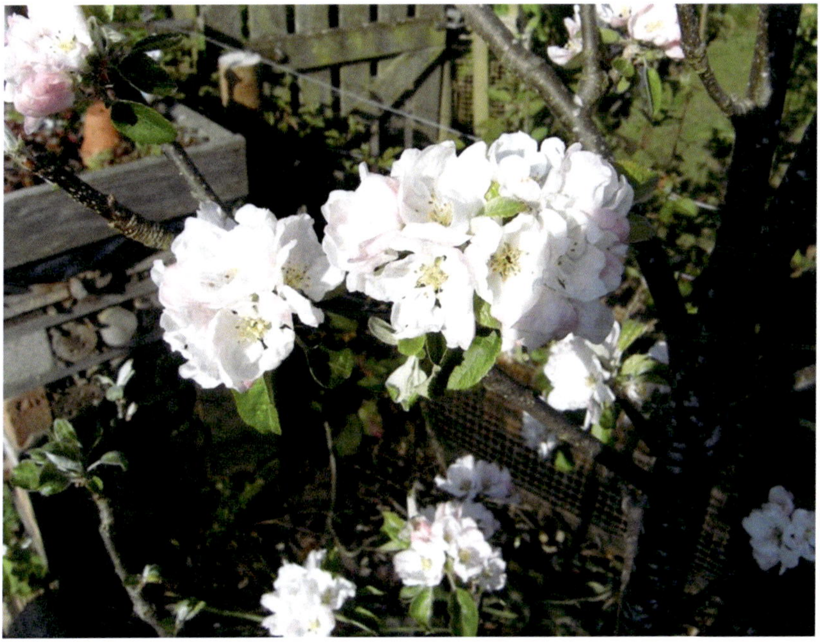

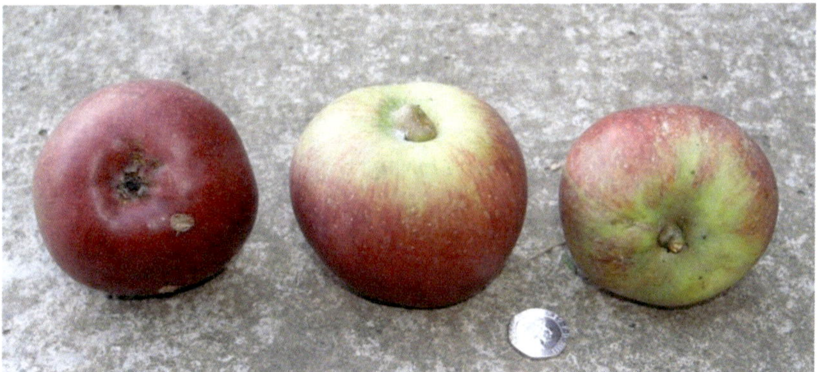

Lord Hindlip

A late dessert apple whose name suggests an origin at Hindlip just north of Worcester, yet it was a Mr Watkins of Hereford who first submitted it to the RHS fruit committee in 1896.

The fruit is medium sized and pearmain like in shape. The skin is flushed with some streaks and a variable level of russet, the flesh is aromatic, crisp, sweet and juicy with a deep cream colour. It has a reputation as a reliable cropper, bearing freely on spurs and, due to its ability to keep until March would have been part of its appeal in the pre refrigerated storage era. It appears in various commercial catalogues of the early 20th century so was perhaps one of the more widely known County varieties.

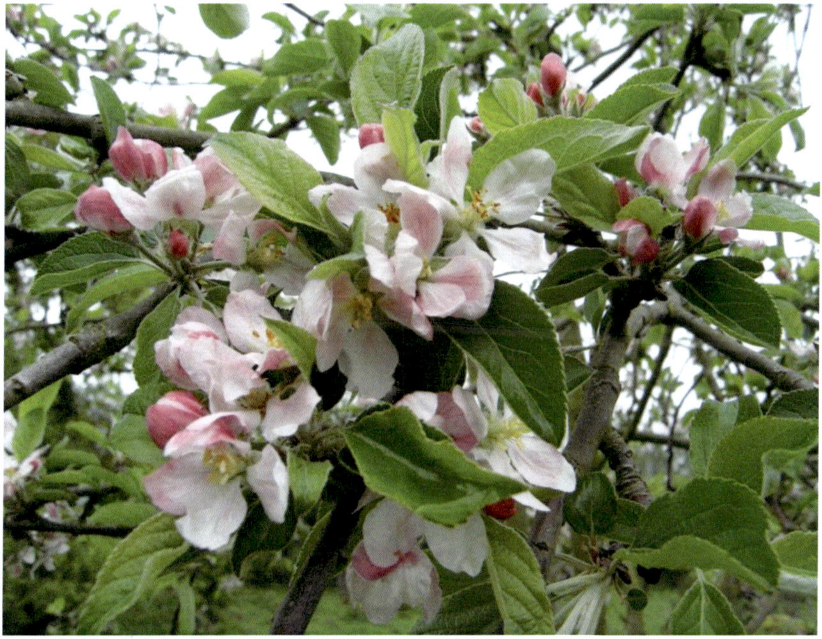

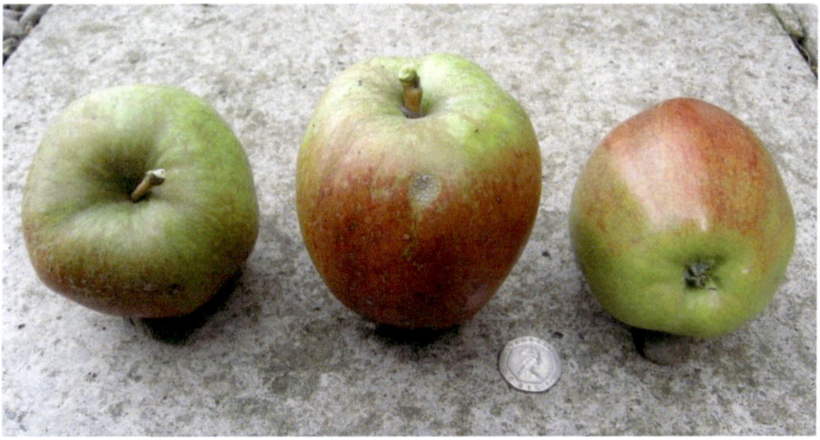

Madresfield Court

Thought to have been raised by William Crump, head gardener of the said Madresfield Court, near Malvern it was first exhibited in 1915 and was then introduced by J. Carless of Worcester. It received an Award of Merit from the Royal Horticultural Society in 1915.

Fruits are large and conical, having a firm, coarse-textured flesh, juicy with a sweet and pleasant aromatic flavour. In a good sunny spot they will ripen to a bright red over a green skin. As a tree it is claimed by some to be a rather shy cropper, but I have found it to crop well as a garden tree.

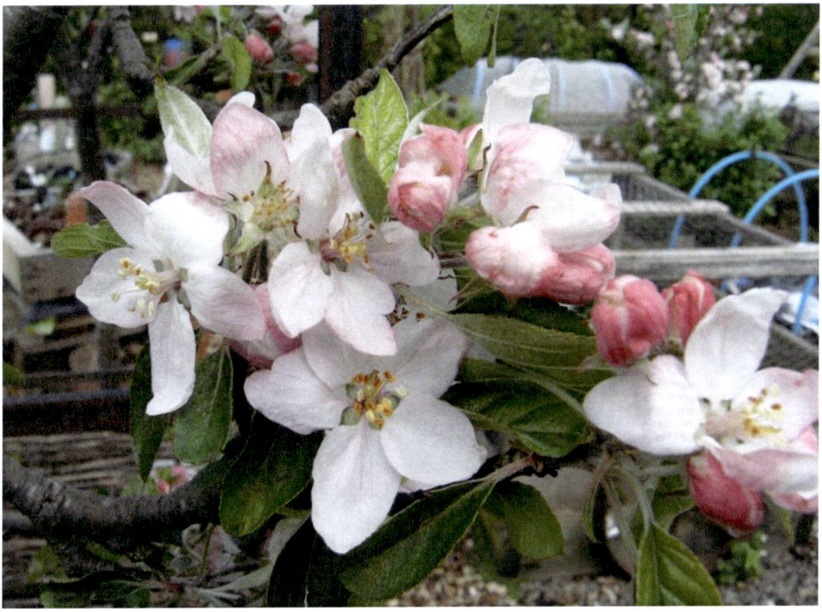

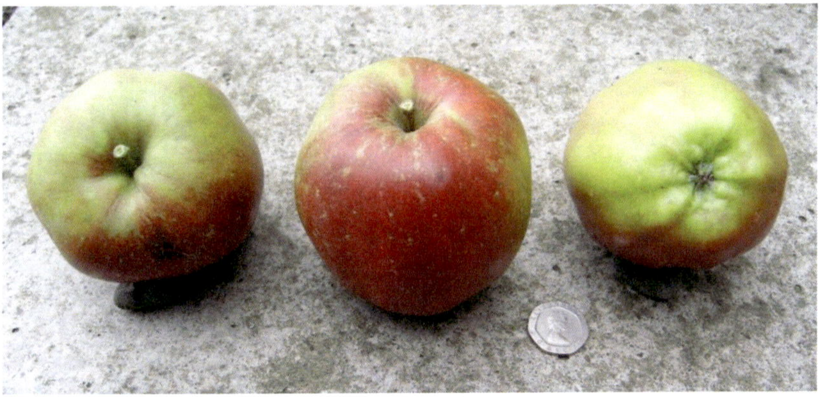

Martin Nonpareil

A medium sized eating apple, said to originate from a Rev George Williams of the village of Martin Hussingtree in 1795. The fruit has a pale green skin turning yellow in storage, with a slightly rough texture and sprinkled with brown russet spots.

Reported to be a vigorous, hardy tree and a good bearer. The apples are supposed to keep until March. This variety was effectively lost until 2012, with no known examples surviving. Following an article in the Martin Hussingtree parish magazine a pair of old trees in a cottage garden came to light and the fruit matched the historical descriptions and illustrations. Recent DNA analysis showed it did not match any other known variety. A few young trees have now been grafted, thus securing the next generation.

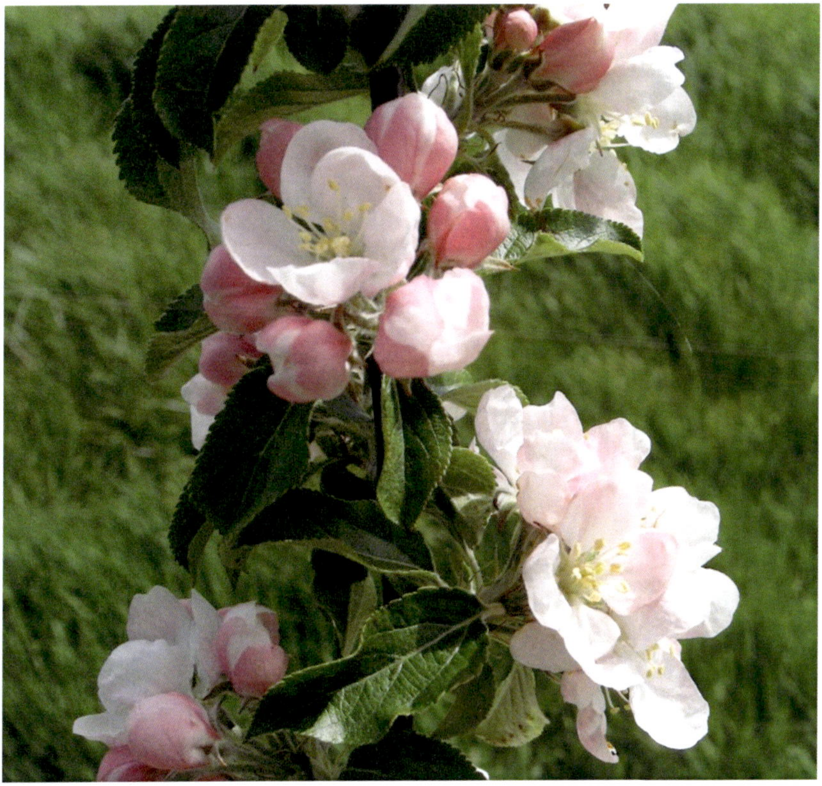

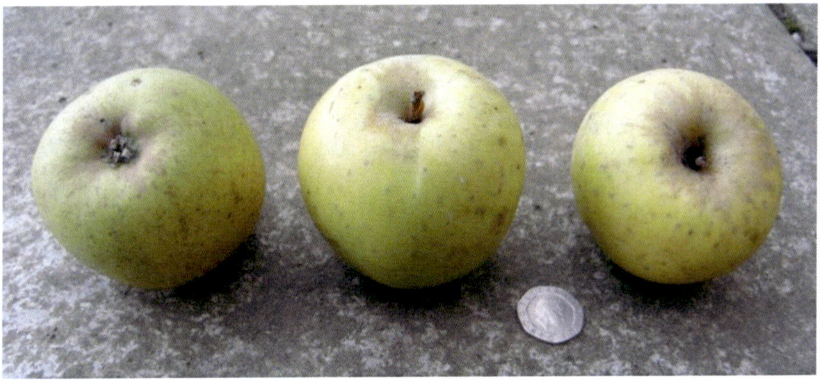

May Queen

Raised by Mr. Haywood of Worcester and first recorded in 1888 when introduced by Messrs. Penwill, it won an RHS award of merit in 1892. This is a fantastic variety and it is hard to see why it is not more popular. An attractive medium sized red dessert apple, it has excellent keeping qualities and will store until April. Certainly on the smaller rootstocks it is amazingly productive and bears well season after season.

According to Bunyard (1920) a neglected fruit of great excellence and as a fruit for small gardens as cordons or bushes it can hardly be surpassed. It is edible from November and keeps excellently. Making but few laterals, pruning is reduced to a minimum, again making it highly suited as a tree for small gardens.

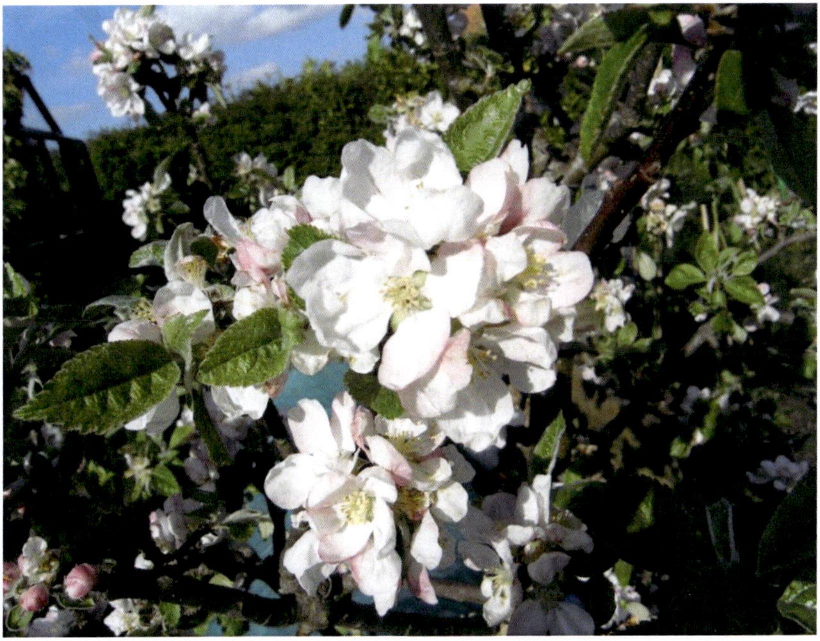

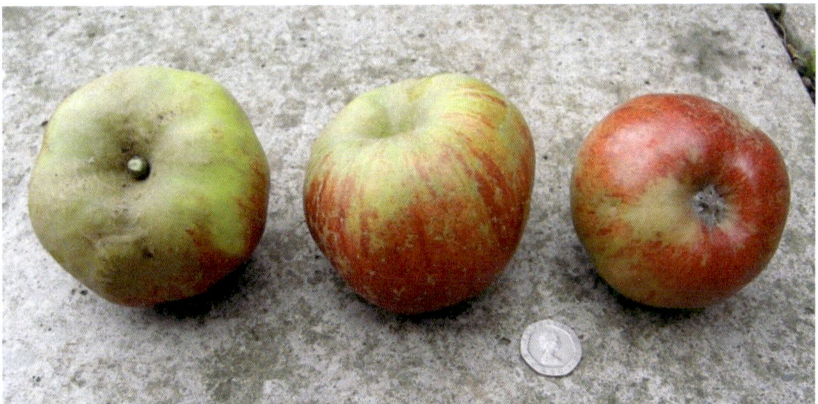

Newland Sack

This variety, as its name indicates, originates form the district of Newland just outside Malvern. According to the Herefordshire Pomona the variety arose around 1800, supposedly from a pip that grew from a discarded pile of pomace (the pulp left over from a cider press) at Newland Court. Recorded as an excellent culinary apple it was said to keep until May without any tendency to decay, even if bruised, a highly unusual characteristic as most varieties rot quickly if damaged. However, after Christmas it was supposed to have sweetened to the point of making it eatable as a dessert apple, so something of a dual purpose variety.

It was exhibited by the RHS in 1888 by William Crump, head gardener at Madresfield Court, the same estate that owned Newland Court. As a tree it is said to be very hardy and a heavy cropper. One of the tenant farmers at Newland Court in the 1800s claimed it was "the best family apple known" and he wished all his orchards were of Newland Sack. Despite these heady days it has long since waned in popularity and is now an extremely rare and obscure variety of the County.

53

Pitmaston Nonpareil

This dessert russet by name claims to be the Pitmaston Russet beyond compare. It was raised at Pitmaston Nursery in Worcester by nurseryman John Williams. It first fruited in 1814 being formally introduced in 1818. The skin is a bright green with varying levels of russet over it, fruits have firm flesh with a rich, aromatic flavour. It will keep up to Christmas and beyond.

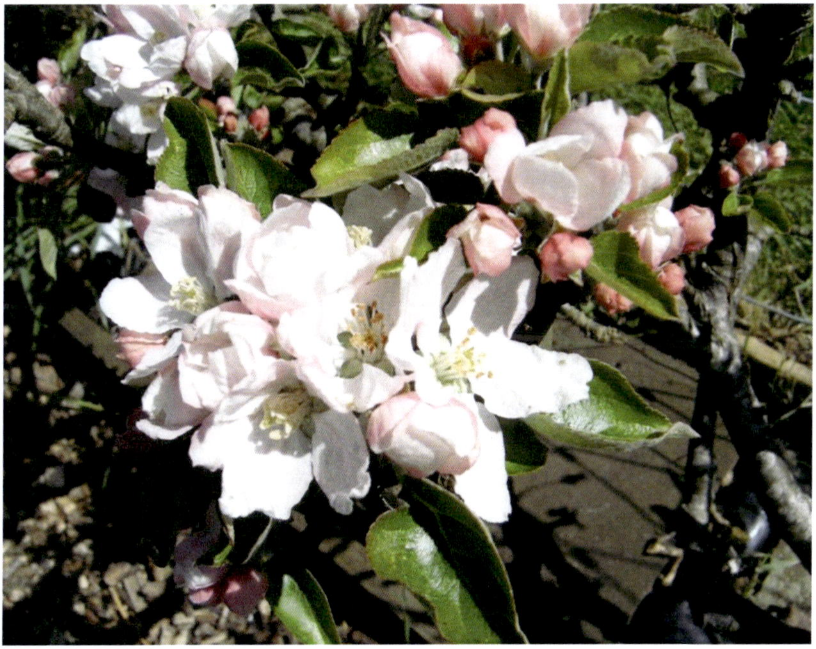

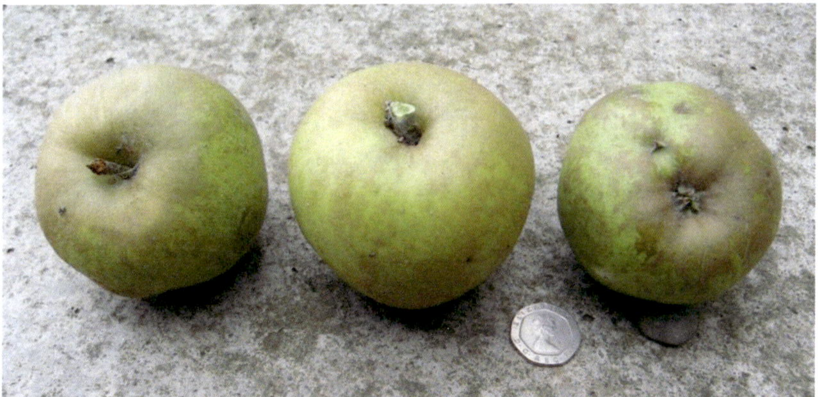

Pitmaston Pine Apple

A quite different and distinctive russet, claimed by Herefordshire, but associated with Pitmaston Nurseries in Worcester. I was first attracted to this particular apple when I read that it is everything the supermarkets hate, being small, yellow and spotty yet with a fantastic taste. It makes for a good garden tree with its moderately vigorous and upright growth pattern. The small fruit are ideal for children, the flesh is crisp, beneath a thick yellow skin with a russet of dots and the flavour is intense, being a sweet, sharp and slightly nutty character with a hint of honey. As a tree it is notably scab resistant although very prone to biennial cropping with huge crops thrown one year and virtually nothing the next, before reverting to another huge crop.

Its origin is speculated to have been from the pip of a Golden Pippin and, although recorded as Hereford 1785, it was introduced by Williams of the Pitmaston Nursery of Worcester, hence its inclusion here. As a tree, a neglected variety because of the apples small size. They are ripe from mid September onwards and if stored well will keep until December.

There is some confusion over the spelling of the name as the early texts have it as Pine Apple where as some modern references have it as Pineapple as in the tropical fruit. I will adhere to the early works as there is no seeming connection to the fruit.

Queen Alexandra

A mid season culinary apple believed to have been raised by William Crump, head gardener at Madresfield Court, Malvern. It was first exhibited in 1902.

The fruit can make a good size, is flat round in shape with yellow green base skin flushed with deep red stripes. A handsome apple that cooks to a brisk, rich puree, making it a very good sauce apple.

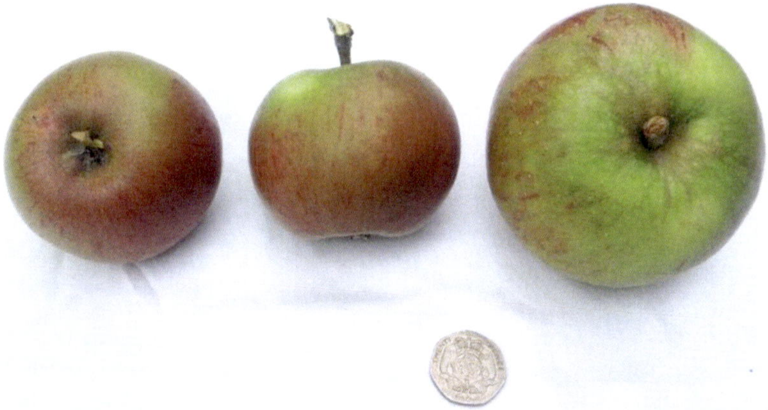

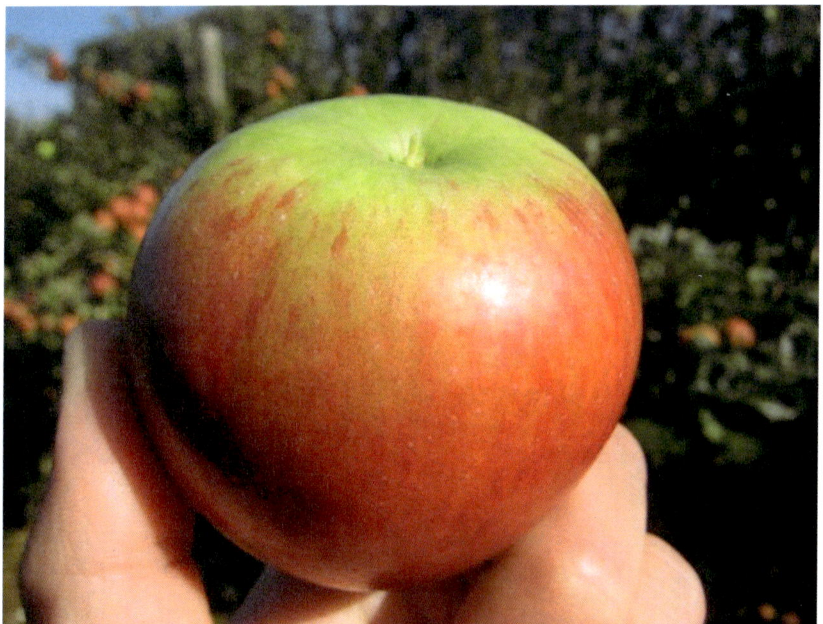

Red Blenheim

A sport and more highly coloured clone of Blenheim Orange that was found at Welland near Malvern in 1966, the fruits have creamy white, somewhat coarse-texture with a rather dry flesh with has a rich, characteristic and an aromatic flavour.

Cooks well as does its namesake although equally a dual purpose which can be eaten from November onwards as a dessert apple.

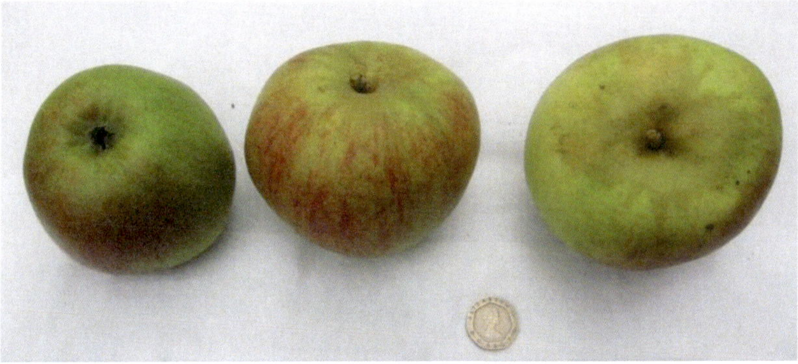

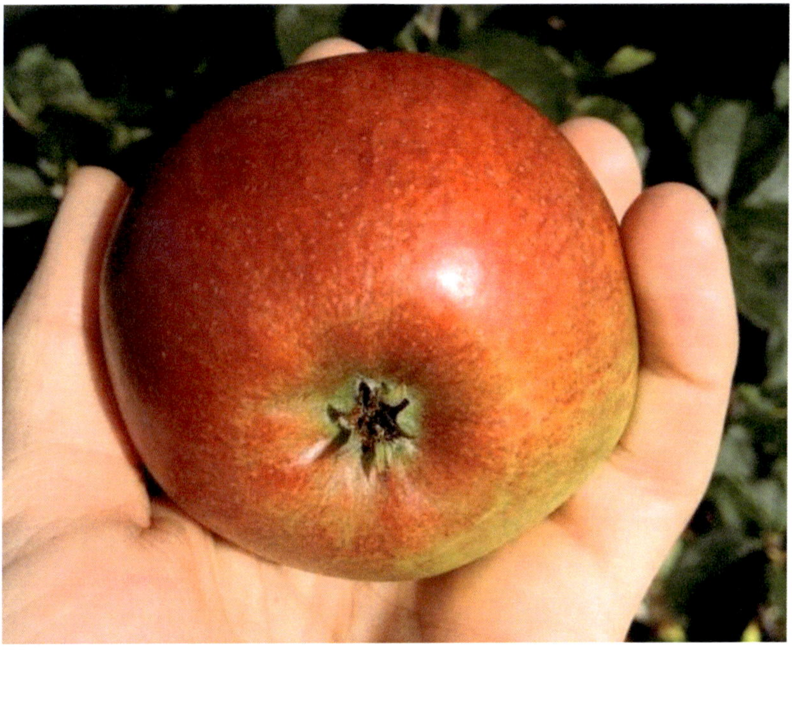

Red Windsor

This modern variety is in fact a stable sport of a German variety, Alkamene, but was found by the late Matt Dalmains of Suckley, Worcestershire. It has gone on to become a major commercial UK mid season variety, with as many as 100,000 trees planted in the last 10 years. It is a very stable sport, very different in appearance and, some say, flavour profile to its parent apple.

A very good cropper, frost hardy with a compact growth, making it an ideal garden tree. It is said to have a Cox like flavour (Cox being one of the parents of Alkemene) yet with a great juicyness. Red Windsor is a licensed variety from Frank P Matthews Ltd, Berrington Court, Tenbury Wells, Worcestershire.

Sandlin Duchess

Raised in about 1880 at Sandlin, Malvern, by H. Gabb, it was introduced to the RHS by William Crump in 1914 and received the award of merit. Crump described it as an "improved Newton Wonder", and, like Newton, it is a good dual purpose variety and can be eaten as a dessert or used as a good culinary apple.

As a tree it exhibits vigorous growth and regular heavy cropping, the fruits have fine, tender, creamy green flesh with a sub acid and slightly sweet flavour. When stewed it breaks down to a well flavoured yellow puree. Ripe from mid-October onwards, if well stored it will keep until February.

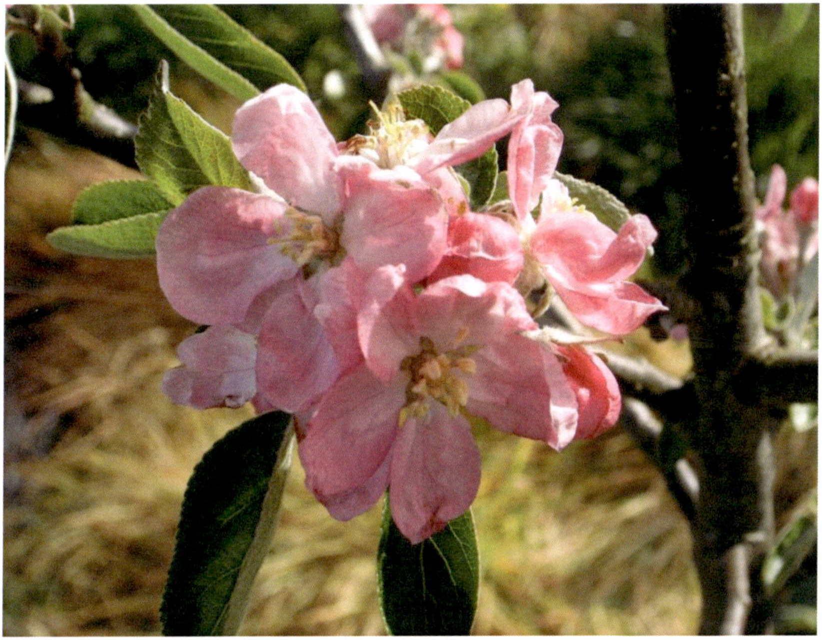

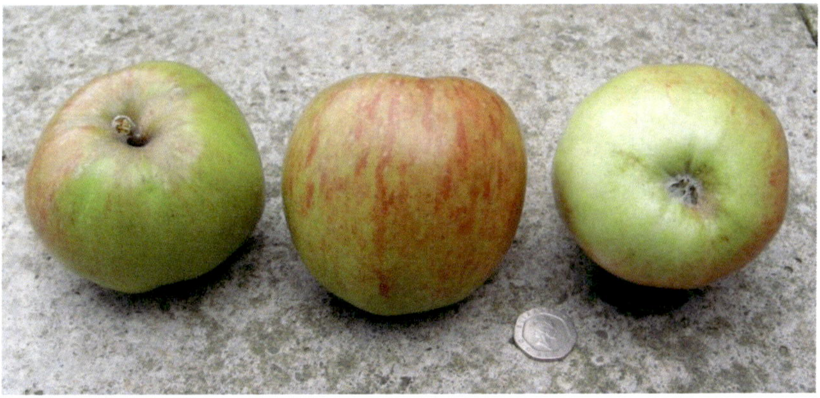

Tupstones

Little is recorded or written anywhere about this obscure apple, first showing up in a 1945 County fruit trial. It is in fact a real gem of a find and has many good qualities, the fruit are attractive with a green and dark red running to almost purple skin colour when ripe, with some russet. The flesh is yellowish white, sweet, firm and possesses a nutty characteristic. It is a good keeper and stored in a cool shed is still very good come February and March. It grows well as a garden tree and forms spurs easily, cropping from the second year onwards on the more dwarfing rootstocks.

Its exact origin or any story concerning it seems absent and where it is listed is simply recorded as Worcestershire.
Of all the heritage varieties of the County this highly obscure variety is a real find and well worth growing in any garden, allotment or orchard.

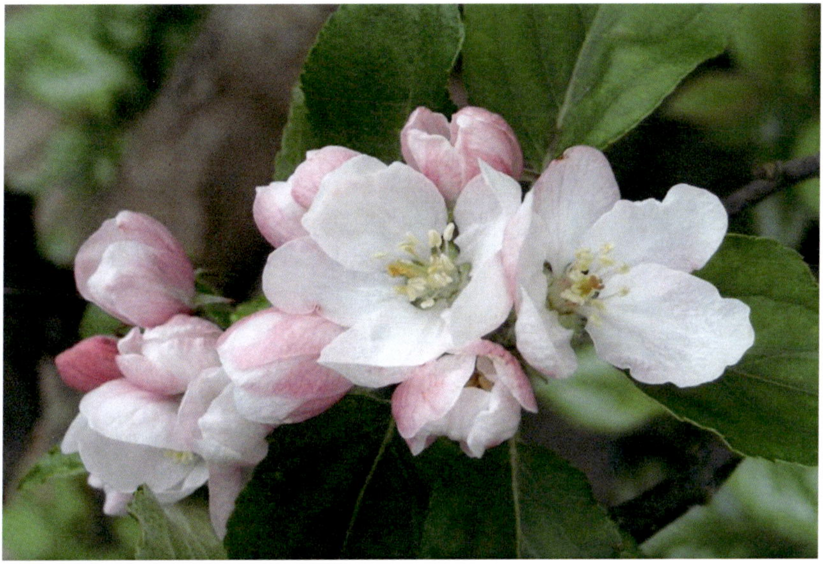

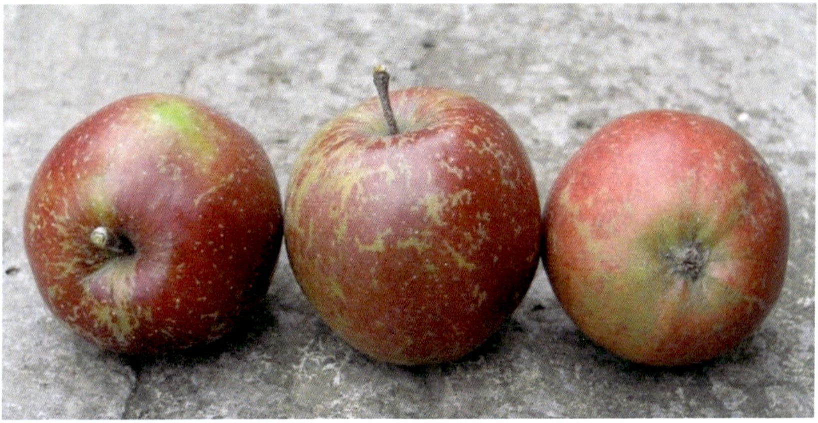

Whiting Pippin

An obscure apple that arose in Worcestershire, recorded in 1883 and said to be much grown in Worcestershire and neighbouring Shropshire in the 19th Century.

Written records or evidence about the variety is limited. Robert Hogg describes it in his Fruit Manual of 1884 and H.V Taylor mentions it briefly in his 1936 The Apples of England as being an apple of Worcestershire.

As a variety it has been the subject of considerable confusion, with some sources claiming it as a culinary apple and others stating it as a dessert. The ones shown here from the author's own collection orchard appear to match Robert Hogg's description pretty accurately. But it still remains a variety of some confusion.

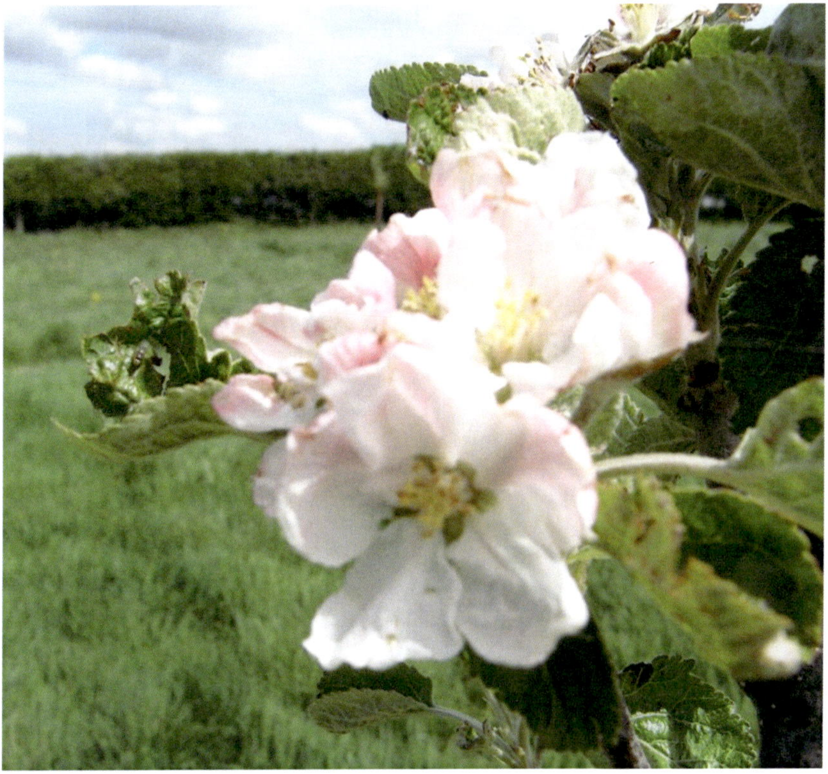

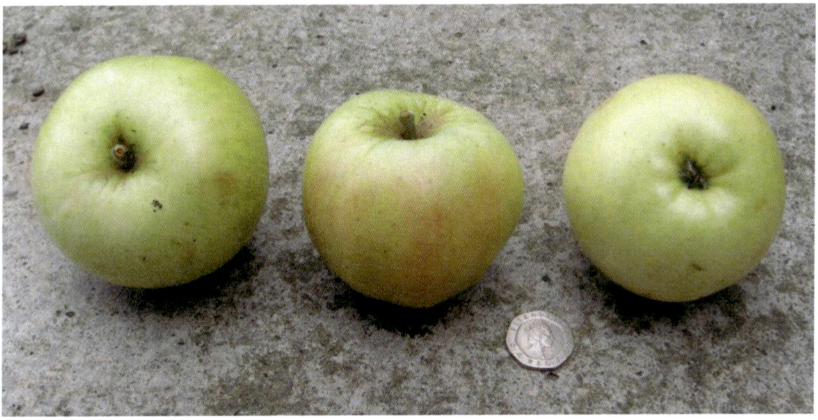

William Crump

This apple takes its name from a Mr William Crump, who was one time head gardener at Madresfield court near Malvern; he is credited with raising it and personally exhibited it in 1908 when it received an RHS Award of Merit. Believed to be a cross between Cox's Orange Pippin and a Worcester Pearmain, it was later exhibited by Earl Beauchamp, also of Madresfield, and won a First Class Certificate in 1910. It was then introduced by Rowe's Nursery of Worcester and is a good quality and attractive looking dessert apple, yet not one you will find commercially available today.

As a tree it has an upright growth habit and seems to do well on a range of rootstocks. The fruit are medium to large and a green to dark red skin colouring, the flesh is firm, crisp and juicy and of good flavour, a nice balance of sweetness and acidity, ripening by mid October with good keeping qualities through until February.

Again one of those varieties that on the face of it has much going for it yet is now comparatively rare, it was claimed one reason it did not gain more popularity was its rather thick skin. However in the author's view is one of the best of the Counties apples and well worth growing.

Worcester Pearmain

Without doubt the most well known of the County's varieties, and the only one still grown on any sort of commercial basis. Believed to have originated from the pip of a Devonshire Quarrenden grown by a Mr Hale of Swan Pool Worcester it was introduced as a commercial variety by Messers Smith of Worcester in 1874. A lovely early dessert apple best eaten straight from the tree in September it will only keep about a month so not one to have in vast quantities, although any surplus could be used to make a fine pinkish apple juice. This variety has been much used in breeding and several other varieties contain it in their parentage. As these were largely bred at research stations they have not been included here, but Tydeman's Early Worcester, Merton Worcester and Laxton's Early Crimson among others are all Worcester Pearmain crosses.

It is described as partial tip bearing in many catalogues, but seems to respond well enough to standard pruning, it makes for a good garden tree and performs well on a range of rootstocks. Said to have a resistance to mildew, yet can be prone to scab in certain summers and can be prone to bird attacks just at the point of ripening. Worth having one in any collection or orchard for its superb taste and its earliness, coming ready before most other dessert apples.

The apples themselves are a round conical and in a warm summer will turn a bright red. They are very sweet, and said to possess a Strawberry like flavour, with a crisp white flesh.

Orchards were once a highly distinctive part of the County landscape

The Lost Varieties

The varieties listed in the previous chapter are those generally considered to be apples which originated here in the County. However, looking further back into history, and in particular to Robert Hogg's Fruit Manual of 1884, several other varieties are mentioned as being from, or of, Worcestershire. Today there is seemingly no trace of some of these apples, there are no known specimens in collections nor are they available from any nursery. However they could still be out there waiting to be rediscovered, still surviving as ancient trees in gardens, hedgerows or some forgotten corner of a field or ancient orchard.

So how do varieties become lost?

Whilst there are well over 2000 named varieties in Britain, it is worth remembering that many of them were never common. The 1800s in particular was a time of a great expansion of horticultural knowledge, and the likes of Robert Hogg travelled the country recording and listing all manner of fruit and vegetables found growing in different regions. However many of these varieties may have only existed within a small area, confined perhaps to a handful of villages. Having originated as a seedling find of some worth, local people would have taken cuttings and propagated and grown it locally, thus there may only ever have been a few tens or low hundreds of some of these regional varieties. Thus with old age, changes in farming and the decline of orchards in the 20th century it was easy for surviving trees to grow old, die or be cut down and with no propagation of young ones, varieties easily became locally extinct. Lost forever as the specific genetic makeup of that variety can never be replicated.

As there are few known illustrations, photos or detailed botanical descriptions of these lost varieties to refer to (Pigeon's Heart, Red Splash and Pitmaston Golden Pippin being exceptions) we have only the 1884 record available to us. Anecdotal reports from the older generation may well be the best - and possibly the only - starting point for those who might be interested in searching out these lost varieties. At the time of going to print the varieties described in the following pages are effectively lost, unless you know differently that is!

Barn Apple – the only known record is an exhibition date of 1883 from Worcester. No other information known.

Jones' Favourite – the only known record of this apple is from 1883 when it was exhibited by a Ritchie of Worcester. Described as a large, conical apple, ribbed with a pale yellow skin and a dry flesh, mid season.

Knott's Kernel – reported in 1884 to have been much grown in the orchards of Worcestershire. This is a striped, medium sized, early season cooking apple. It is roundish if slightly flattened in shape, with skin said to be citron coloured and considerably covered in dark purplish stripes. It has a crisp juicy flesh with a brisk acidity.

Pigeon's Heart - recorded in 1861 from Smith of Worcester. Said to be a large to medium-sized cooking apple with yellowish-green skin flushed with brown streaks and red russet dots. The flesh is crisp and tinged green and the flavour sub acid. It harvests very late and is said to keep until May.
It is highly likely that this is fact the variety described in the Herefordshire Pomona of 1885 as Pigeon and in the National Fruit Collection, Brogdale as Pigeon de Jerusalem. If so then its origin is unknown (possibly French) and seems to be a once reasonably widely grown cooking apple known by a range of synonyms involving the word pigeon.

Red Splash – said to have been widely grown in the Newland area of Malvern and surrounding parishes and sold mainly to the producers of pickles, chutneys and apple jellies. A small apple of about two inches in size, golden-yellow skin with extensive crimson streaks. Hogg refers to it also being known by the name of New Bromley, but equally this name does not relate to any known variety around today, whilst the Herefordshire Pomona of 1870 includes it as a cider apple.

Sitchampton Russet - a medium sized eating apple with a skin of grey russet with brownish flush. The flesh is crisp, tender and yellowish and the flavour is aromatic. It keeps well until February. It may also have once been called Sitchampton Pearmain. No reference to it appears anywhere else, so it could be a case of a local name for some other variety, such as Golden Russet or Aromatic Russet both mentioned in the Herefordshire Pomona of 1885. Or it could be a local seedling russet that was propagated in and around the village, and the few trees that there may once have been are now long gone.

Pitmaston Golden Wreath - a tiny yellow crab apple originating from J Williams Esq. of Pitmaston, Worcester. Said to be a cross between Golden Pippin and Siberian Crab.

Pitmaston Golden Pippin - a small, yellow desert apple, seemingly similar to Pitmaston Pineapple if the description is to be believed. Again originating from Williams Nursery in Pitmaston. It is described and illustrated in the Herefordshire Pomona of 1885.

Woodshill Apple – said to have originated in Woodshill orchard in the district of Bromsgrove it went on to become an excellent fruit, being widely cultivated in the local area.

There are also several other references to varieties with a suggested link to the City or County:

Worcester Apple - listed by John Rea in his Flora, Ceres & Pomona III in 1660, only known record.

Worcester Fillbasket - in existence 1888 only record.

Golden Worcester - described in 1831, still in existence in 1872, small, intermediate shape, rectangular, convex, not ribbed, skin gold slightly tinged red, flesh firm yellow; season late to very late; knobbed stalk and prominent eye.

Worcester Beauty - is a variety grown commercially in New Zealand today.

Worcester Russet - in existence 1853 only record.

Worcestershire Russet - in existence 1864 only record.

Early Worcester appears to be a synonym of Tydeman's Early Worcester.

All the above pre date the introduction of Worcester Pearmain in 1875 so suggest some other association with the City.

Lengthier and far more detailed descriptions of some of these varieties can be found in Robert Hogg's The Fruit Manual of 1884, which is still in print: ISBN 1-904078-03-6.

It is worth noting that Worcester Pearmain has long been a favoured variety in apple breeding and is one of the parents of a number of other varieties. As such the Worcester characteristics can be found in other apples which can lead to much head scratching when trying to identify unknown apples that appear to "somewhat Worcester like"

The varieties Merton Worcester (1914) and Tydeman's Early Worcester (1929) are not included in this volume as they were bred elsewhere, and the name association is simply that Worcester Pearmain is in their parentage.

Worcester Pearmain has been widely crossed to breed other varieties some of which are very similar in appearance,

Pears

Despite the title of this book and its overwhelming focus on apples, it would seem wrong not to include something on pears, especially the Worcester Black Pear, so synonymous with the County. There are very few pears with a claim of origin in Worcestershire so the few there are, are included here.

The Worcester Black Pear (or Black Worcester)

The iconic Worcester Black Pear appears today in places such as the city coat of arms, the County Council crest and the Cricket Club badge, whilst an image of the pear blossom was borne as a badge by the Worcestershire Yeomanry Cavalry until 1956. The earliest reference to any pear associated with a crest is in relation to the Worcestershire Bowmen, depicting a pear tree laden with fruit on their banners at the battle of Agincourt in 1415. Drayton's poem of Agincourt mentions the fruit, where it is referred to as the badge of Worcester: "Wor'ster a pear tree laden with its fruit".

Tradition has it that during the visit of Queen Elizabeth I to Worcester in 1575 she saw a pear tree laden with black pears, which had been moved from the gardens at White Ladies and re-planted in her honour by the gate through which the queen was to enter the city. Noticing the tree Elizabeth is said to have directed the City to add three pears to its coat of arms.

The Worcester Black Pear may originally have been introduced into the country by the Romans and was possibly first recorded from Warden Abbey in Bedfordshire in the 13th Century. It is the oldest surviving cultivar of pears of its type, a group to which the name 'warden' or 'wardon' pears was given. It is possibly the same cultivar as the French pear 'de Livre'.

Worcestershire history and place names are littered with references to pears, indicating their past cultural and economic importance to the region. The counties of Worcestershire, Herefordshire and Gloucestershire were the focus of pear introduction to England by the Normans and they have been cultivated ever since. Seedlings from the original trees gave rise to specific varieties for eating, cooking and the production of Perry.

Large Worcester Black Pear trees are distinctive within the landscape, growing up to 50ft (15m) tall with a long, relatively narrow crown. The ageing bark has a square checkerboard pattern and in spring the trees are covered with a cascade of white blossom. They are found scattered across the county in old orchards, hedgerows and gardens, often being planted on the windward side of orchards or fields to provide shelter. The trees were commonly grafted onto wild pear rootstock which made them very vigorous, hence the great height they achieved.

Whilst the Black Pear is not now grown commercially it has numerous characteristics to recommend it for this: it is easily cultivated, needs little attention, does well on most soils and has a long life span, good disease resistance and prolific fruit bearing capacity. They also have a pleasing and impressive appearance and their stature makes them suitable for use as a nurse crop or shelter for other orchard trees.

Throughout the 1990s and 2000s Worcestershire County Council made Black Pears available through its Fruit Trees for Worcestershire scheme and several hundred young trees were planted. Now available from local nurseries on a quince rootstock it can be grown as a smaller tree so making it better suited to gardens and other small sites.

The Black Pear is a cooking or culinary pear which is oval and irregular in shape. Individual fruits can be up to 78mm (3") wide and 85mm long, weighing as much as 260g. They have a dark mahogany colour (not true black) with russet freckles and small areas of rough skin. The flesh is a pale yellow or cream, tinged green under the skin. A common mistake is to pick the fruit in October or early November and to try to use it immediately, when it is crisp, hard and gritty. They should instead be stored until January and will then keep until April. It was this quality of keeping through the winter without refrigeration that once made them so valuable. Various varieties of Warden Pears were supposedly transported with the troops as part of their food provisions because of their long lasting properties.

How to cook a Black Pear

As far back as the 13th Century the "Warden" pear was a baking pear of great repute and was for centuries a favourite for inclusion in pies and pastries, described in every early cookery book. In early literature the warden was considered a distinct type of fruit and lists of fruit varieties included both pears and wardens. Wardon pears in syrup were served in the same course as venison, quail, sturgeon, fieldfare and other high quality dishes. Recipes from a 1450 cookery book include meat and fish cooked with pears, leeks, small onions or garlic sauce.

Hot baked wardens:
 6 large firm pears
 ½ – ¾ pint / 300 – 450ml red wine
 1oz / 28g brown sugar
 Pinch of ground cinnamon, ginger and saffron

Peel the pears and place in an oven proof dish. Mix the red wine with the brown sugar and spices and pour over the pears. Bake in the oven at 180 C / 350 F / Gas Mark 4 until tender (this can be up to 2 hours in the case of black pears).

Pitmaston Duchess

Raised in 1841 by John Williams of Pitmaston, Worcester, it was once considered the premier pear for canning and bottling. A magnificent looking pear that can make great sizes, rarely less than 12oz and even up to 28oz. The sweet lemony flesh with its melting almost buttery texture was much prized and, as such, the variety was cultivated across the UK and into northern Europe. At the London Pear conference of 1895 George Bunyard considered it "the best and finest market pear" and it was still planted as a commercial variety up until the 1950s.
Whilst no longer a commercial variety, well worth growing in gardens and allotments as a great all round pear.

Judge Amphlett

This small Perry pear is named after a Worcester assizes court judge and one of the founders of Worcester Cricket Club. How he ended up with a pear named after him is unclear. First documented in the early 1900s, the fruit is small in size, skin is yellow or greenish with an occasional flush on the sunny side and considerable russet around the stem and the eye.
Now considered rare, the tree grows in the classic upright champagne flute shape so distinctive of perry pears.

Clues from History

As has been stated, many of these local or heritage varieties were distinct to a specific locality; village or district. It is hard to gauge if they were just a local variety shared amongst villagers and or to what extent they were ever more widely available or grown. Some of them did catch on and were propagated and made available by nurseries of the day. Interestingly in the report of the Apple and Pear Conference of 1888 held in Greenwich, in the Worcestershire section it only makes reference to five of the County varieties, as being among those recommended by County growers. Worcester Pearmain, May Queen, Pitmaston Russet, Newland Sack and Rushock Pearmain (King Charles Pearmain).

As this was the period regarded by many as the height of apple growing culture and interest in varieties, it does rather point to the prospect that many of the County varieties were never widespread or well known outside their specific localities. One way to try and gauge their spread is to see what varieties were being offered by the fruit nurseries of the day. Virtually all the large, once renowned, fruit nurseries of this area are long gone, part of a world that has passed. The catalogues from some of them can be found in archives and the second hand book trade; they offer an insight into what were considered the notable varieties of the day.

For example in the 1921 catalogue of the famous King's Acre Nurseries, out of 139 apple varieties being offered only five of the Worcestershire varieties are listed; Chatley's Kernel, Lord Hindlip, Gladstone, William Crump and Worcester Pearmain. Whilst a Richard Smith & Co of Worcester catalogue of the early 1900 offers 147 varieties only four of which are from the County; Chatley's Kernel, Lord Hindlip, Gladstone and Worcester Pearmain. Again pointing to the possibility that many of the County varieties were never commercial.

Whilst John Weathers in his 1913 Commercial Gardening states that the apples chiefly grown in Worcestershire are Worcester Pearmain,

Devonshire Quarrenden, Ecklinville, Lord Derby, Lord Grosvenor, Stirling Castle, Cox's Orange Pippin, Lane's Prince Albert and Allington Pippin. So only one County variety among those.

From my own observations of surveying old Orchards, amongst the commonest finds of old trees are Bramley's, Newton Wonders, Lord Derby, Grenadier, Worcester Pearmain, Blenheim Orange, Warner's King and Tom Putts. These appear to be among the popular commercial varieties of 100 odd years ago they were the Gala, Braeburn and Pink Lady of their day.

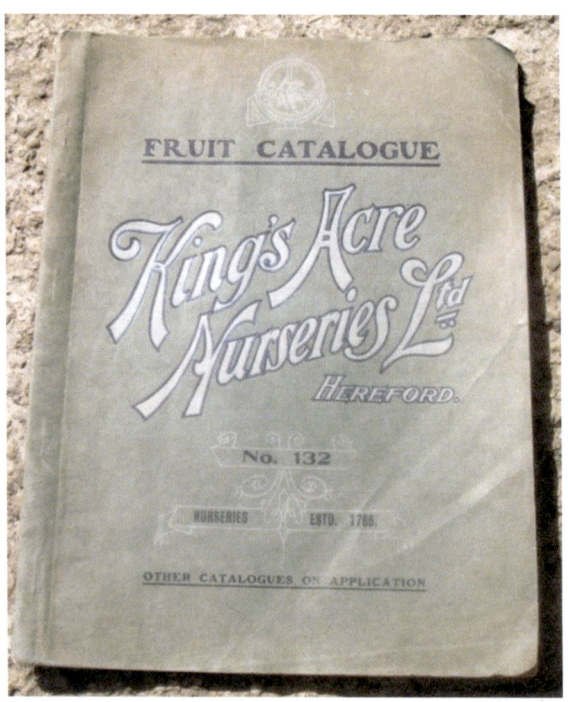

King's Acre Nurseries 1921 catalogue a useful source of gauging what was popular at that time.

Orchard Stories

There is a rich vein of tales, stories and anecdotes surrounding orchards and fruit growing in the County. The trouble with the stories of apple provenance and, in particular, their references in literature, is that most of the reference works cite previous works as their source. Any mistake, inaccuracy or just made up tale therefore has the potential to be perpetuated down the years and taken as truth.

Robert Hogg's works in the mid and late 1800s are the source of a vast number of references for varietal names, yet we know little about Hogg's research methods or the samples on which he based his descriptions and stories. The following tales offer interesting historical insights into the naming of fruit varieties (including examples of how names can be claimed by more than one area and more than one tale) and some of the niche markets developed for fruit produce.

The Name Remains

So many orchards have gone and so often the only clue is in the name. How many Orchard Closes and Orchard Drives are there on modern housing estates where an orchard once stood? Equally all the large old 18th Century nurseries have gone, In Blakedown the site of the original nursery was built upon in the early 2000s and, interestingly, the apple they were famous for introducing in 1868 appears to have lived on in the street name of the road into the estate.

One wonders how many of the residents are aware of the apple association of their address?

Scotch Bridget

An apple, a barmaid and a Tenbury Tale

The apple Scotch Bridget, according to most references, originates from the Scottish borders in about 1851. Yet there persists in the Teme Valley a rather different story, claiming its origins in Tenbury Wells. It was believed in the 1920s and 30s that the variety had originated from a seedling in the garden of the Swan Hotel in Tenbury Wells and that it had been named after a Scottish barmaid by the name of Bridget who worked at the hotel at the time. The date of the apple's discovery and naming seem unclear but it was in Hogg's book of 1851 and was extensively grown in Worcestershire in the early 1900s, so it would have to have been some decades before that.

David Spilsbury of Eastham claims his father always believed it to be a Teme Valley apple, until he visited Lancashire in the 1950s and found orchards of it growing up near Blackpool and was truly surprised at finding it in cultivation in another county. There are also accounts of it being grown over the channel in France and Germany but again tying up the dates in sequence seems difficult. Its spread into other counties and even countries is easily possible, as once established a named and reputable variety would quickly spread through the nursery trade, but who had it first and where it actually originated is unclear.

As an apple its appeal was undoubtedly its keeping qualities. It is a very dry apple with a low juice content and good specimens will keep through winter until April and May, so prior to refrigerated storage and supermarket distribution it would have been a valuable keeping apple through the long winter months.

Scotch Bridgets in April, the keeping quality was a large part of their appeal

It is interesting none the less how this type of story springs up. The truth may never be known but it is rather appealing that a girl from up north, a long way from home, could have had an apple named in her honour by the folk of Tenbury Wells. Alternatively it may have been an already established variety, possibly from Scotland, when a comment in a Tenbury pub to a girl called Bridget, to the effect of 'did they call this apple after you?' was misheard and perpetuated as a local story…who knows?

The Princess Pippin
A royal visit and what's in a name

Many apple varieties have several names or synonyms and can be known by different names in different districts or counties. In Tenbury Wells there is a story with royal associations surrounding an apple that went on to be known as the Princess Pippin.

In 1832 the young Princess (later Queen) Victoria visited the town and during her stay was presented with a basket of apples of a type known locally as Stanardines. She duly took them with her and was reputedly so impressed that a message came back instructing that they be known from then on as the Princess Pippin. It was subsequently grown on a significant scale in the area for decades afterwards and known by that name.

The origin of the original seemingly odd name Stanardine is unclear; however it appears to be a local name for a far more widespread apple. Following detailed examination, the Teme Valley Apple Group are convinced that what is known as the Stanardine or Princess Pippin in Tenbury, is the same apple known elsewhere as King of The Pippins and Shropshire Pippin.

This story is validated by a 1932 article in the Tenbury paper marking 100 years since Victoria's visit and citing the Hereford Times write up of it a century earlier. As an apple it was still found on an extensive scale until the 1950s, growing in the Teme Valley, and it is a good mid-season eating apple. There are a few locals who still claim the Princess Pippin / Stanardine to be two different apples, but anatomically it seems the same and it is always worth remembering that soil type, altitude, levels of sunshine and general growing position can alter the taste and appearance of the same variety.

The Mincemeat Man
A tale of a real niche market

There is a story of farmers in the Teme Valley growing the apple Collington Bittersweet (also known as Collington Big Bitters) for the mincemeat market, bought up once a year by a particular buyer and shipped off direct to the factory. This variety is actually a cider apple but its firm chunky flesh would hold together when cooked. According to David Spilsbury of Eastham, Newton Wonder could also be used for mincemeat as it has similar properties of holding together during the cooking process.

The Home Orchard

There is a clear distinction to make between a commercial orchard growing apples for market and the small or home orchard producing fruit for domestic consumption. To make a commercial orchard you need large numbers of the same variety in order to obtain a large enough crop to sell, in order to maximise labour effectively this monoculture all comes ripe together, so minimising transport and picking time.

In the case of domestic fruit production the opposite is true, a glut is the last thing the homeowner or small holder wants. Rather a steady stream of fruit is preferred, each subsequent variety coming ready as the previous one ends, some for eating in the season, others for storing through the winter. Hence the more diverse an old orchard is the less likely it was ever very commercial. Some of the larger orchards grew five or six different varieties in order to supply the market from September to December. In this case many multiples of each variety would have been grown to make a viable crop, this pattern of perhaps a couple of rows of each can still be found in a few remnant orchards. Whereas an old orchard with one or two trees of lots of different varieties is more likely to have just been a farm or small holding orchard producing fruit for domestic consumption.

When planning a home orchard today, research is the key, do a lot of investigating before you purchase and plant. In the case of apples, one would look for a nice early season eater coming ready in August / early September, followed by a second early ready in mid to late September, then an October ripening eater and then two or three varieties that will keep through the winter. Thus the availability of fresh apples to the homeowner is maximised.

Aftercare

Whilst it was never the intention of this book to be a 'how' to guide to orchard management, as it encourages the planting of these heritage varieties it is worth a brief mention of the best practice when planting. All too often young trees of all sorts are planted with the best of intentions and then neglected or at the very least not looked after.

Aftercare is the key to the successful establishment of any tree, young trees need to be well maintained and that can mean preventing grass and other vegetation from establishing around the base of the tree and thus competing with its roots for nutrients and moisture. Physical protection is also needed for rabbits, deer or anything that would eat your tree. A tree is not just for planting, it needs looking after for a good number of years so as to give it the best possible start in life.

A well established young tree with guard and weed free root zone.

The Future

So what of the future?

There has been a real upsurge of interest in aspects of food production, many people are really interested in where things come from and what is local. In the case of the apple so much is owed to Common Ground and that initial work back in the early 1990s that kick started it all.

We will not see a situation where these County varieties appear on the supermarket shelves, for they will never satisfy the uniformity of the mass market. We can however celebrate and grow these varieties in our gardens, allotments and small holdings and in so doing eat and enjoy a variety of apples and pears that the mass market can never compete with.

Much is owed to regional apple groups like the Marcher Apple Network who have done so much to rediscover and preserve many of our heritage varieties, and to the enthusiasts and specialist Nurseries who have propagated these varieties so that we can again access them.

So it is with the amateurs and the enthusiasts, the home growers and the allotmenteers with whom the future of these varieties rests. The genetic variation they contain is well worth preserving in a world of the ever more homogenised and uniform. We may need their diversity in terms of resilience and disease resistance in a changing future.

So when selecting a tree a to plant in your garden, go for something local, something unusual…. something special.

Acknowledgments

I am grateful to a host of people who freely shared their knowledge, enthusiasm and stories.

In particular David Spilsbury for his knowledge and encouragement in this project. Also John Edwards, Reg Farmer, Brian Roberts and Alec Wall of the Teme Valley Apple Group.

To Nick Dunn, Tim Dixon and John Edgeley for imparting their knowledge down the years, to the committee of the Marcher Apple Network for their encouragement and to Andrew Morton for his encouragement and assistance in research.

To Karen Humphries and Paul Esrich and the Three Counties Orchard Project and the Heritage Lottery Fund for funding the initial publication costs.

To Lorinda Jewsbury of the National Fruit Collection at Brogdale for being most helpful with my enquiries.

To Phil and Lauren for assistance in photography at Brogdale.

To Peter Weekes for permission to photograph apples in his orchard.

To the Kemerton Conservation Trust, and John Clarke in particular, for his co-operation and permission to photograph some of the KTC collection.

To Sue Clifford and Angela King of Common Ground without whom this whole interest in the local distinctiveness and mapping local varieties would likely as not never have come about.

Finally to my family, Rachel and the children, Eva and Nils, for putting up with my eccentric apple obsession all these years.

Here is hoping it rubs off on the children, we need a next generation to keep this subject alive and pippin!

References

Common Ground. 2000. The Common Ground book of Orchards

Hogg.R. 1884. The Fruit Manual, Langford Press

Lindley.J. 1888. The Pomologia Britannica, London

Morgan J & Richards A. 1993. The New Book of Apples, Ebury press

Porter.M. The Welsh Marches Pomona, The Marcher Apple Network

Sanders.R. 2010. The Apple Book, Frances Lincoln Ltd

Smith.M.W.G 1971 The National Apple Register of the United Kingdom, Ministry of Agriculture Fisheries and Food, London

Taylor,H.V. 1936 The Apples of England, Crosby Lockwood & Sons ltd

Weathers.J. 1913. Commercial Gardening.

Catalogue King's Acre Nursery Ltd 1921

The Apple and Pear Conference Report of 1888.

Apples of the Welsh Marches 2002, Marcher Apple Network

About the Author

Despite the title of this book Wade Muggleton actually lives just across the border in Shropshire where he has over 100 varieties of apple growing in his own collection including nearly all those in this book. He has worked as a College Lecturer in Cambridgeshire teaching countryside management and for the last 17 years as a Countryside Officer in Worcestershire. He writes and teaches on the subject of Orchards, fruit and gardening.